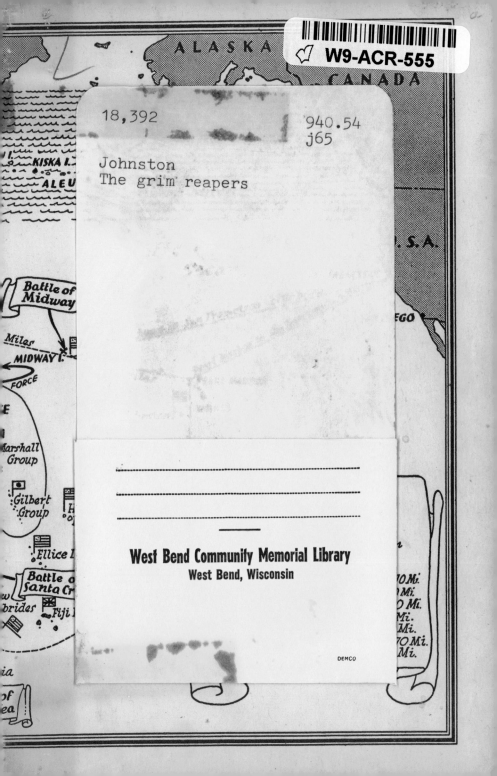

THE GRIM REAPERS

PRODUCING BOOKS IN WARTIME

This book has been produced in conformity with war-time economy standards.

The amount of reading matter has in no way been curtailed—when necessary more words per page are used.

Thinner books and smaller books will save paper, cloth, metals, transportation and storage space and will conserve manpower.

The publishers will do their utmost in meeting the objectives of the War Production Board towards the successful prosecution of the war.

STANLEY JOHNSTON *has also written*

QUEEN OF THE FLAT-TOPS: THE U. S. S. *Lexington*
AND THE CORAL SEA BATTLE

"This complete account of the Coral Sea Battle is the most coherent eyewitness story of any sea battle that this reviewer has ever read."—W. L. Duffus, *New York Times Book Review*

"No American can read this tale of the Lexington's last hours without experiencing a deep sense of pride in the American fighting man and without realizing anew that the spiritual essentials of victory are possessed in abundance by the American Nation."—*Christian Science Monitor*

"This reviewer remains overwhelmed by Mr. Johnston's inexhaustible energy, good fortune, and competence as a reporter. He has told a great story."
—*Atlantic Monthly*

"Altogether, QUEEN OF THE FLAT-TOPS is a war book that is more exciting than any fiction we have ever read."—*New York Daily News*

E. P. DUTTON & COMPANY, INC.

THE
GRIM REAPERS

By
STANLEY JOHNSTON

Published by THE BLAKISTON COMPANY, *Philadelphia*

Distributed by E. P. DUTTON & CO., INC., *New York*

CONTENTS

DEDICATED TO

LEPPLA, MEAD, RHODES, CALDWELL,
DAVIS, FULTON, BARNES, MILLER,
EDWARDS AND VON LEHE—THE REAPERS
WHO DID NOT RETURN.

ACKNOWLEDGMENT

I am grateful to the *Chicago Tribune* for their permission to incorporate in this volume some of their copyrighted material from the newspaper series about the Grim Reapers.

PREFACE

In the years immediately before this war began, the picture of the coming conflict painted most frequently by experts was one of battles waged by masses of men and machines against similar masses. There would be no place for the individual; a hero like Sergeant York wouldn't be possible.

But the second World War has turned out differently. On more than one occasion, the skill of a man or a small group of men has accomplished feats which contributed greatly to winning victories or staving off defeats in minor engagements, and in giving the edge to one side or the other in major battles.

It is a war of machines, indeed, but one in which each machine depends on a man, or crews of men, and where the destructive power of each weapon is increased in direct ratio to the skill and audacity of those who control and direct it. Thus the age of machine war is not only dependent on individuals, but it has given individuals a fighting power far in excess of that possessed by other fighting men in other wars of the past.

If I appear to imply in the following pages that a particular man, group or vessel is better than another in valor, spirit and accomplishment, it is wholly unintentional. My primary reason for singling out the experiences and performances of VF-10, the Grim Reapers, is simply that I followed the formation of this squadron from its first stages, when Commander James H. Flatley drew up plans for it on the overcrowded transport which brought survivors of the Coral Sea engagement back to American ports, right up to the time Commander Flatley was detached from the squadron to take over command of an entire air group, now "somewhere in the Pacific."

If Commander Flatley seems to take a place of preference, it is because I knew him better than the other flyers, and because Jim, during his too short spell ashore from sea duty, unselfishly spent many hours furnishing me with material and data on his squadron's actions—hours he might otherwise have spent at leisure with his family. I owe him most sincere thanks for his thorough help and untiring efforts to supply background and general information about his squadron mates.

The flyers who make up the Grim Reapers are duplicated many times over, in scores and scores of other air squadrons. We are fortunate in possessing men of their caliber, and in numbers, for in them lies our strength.

STANLEY JOHNSTON

In Tribute

To the superb officers and men under the sea, and on the sea, and in the air, who have during the past days performed such magnificent feats for the United States. Your names have been written in golden letters on the pages of history and you have won the everlasting gratitude of your countrymen. No honor for you could be too great and my pride in you is beyond expression. Magnificently done. To the glorious dead—hail heroes and rest with God. God bless all of you.

> —ADMIRAL WILLIAM HALSEY, Commander of the Fleet, to all ships in the South Pacific and all commanding generals, on November 17th, 1942

Each officer and man of this group has shown fine aggressive spirit and unflinching courage; and, which is also highly important, kept up superb morale along with it.

We have, as we all hoped we would, borne out in grand style the predictions in the Group Commander's memorandum of October 6th, upon first embarking aboard this carrier which led to Santa Cruz, and of November 2nd, upon sailing for Guadalcanal, i.e., that the Navy would know of us, and that the Japs would regret our very existence.

Your country and your Navy are proud of you and I hope you are each relaxed for a moment and enjoying justly earned self-pride in your victory.

But let us pause in our justifiable yet sober relaxation and salute those comrades of our group we have lost. God rest their sturdy souls after the supreme job they have done so well for the greatest of all causes.

We of the group who were not able to follow through all the Lunga action will yet have chances to repeat our: "Ten for one, Group Ten punch!" for other knockouts.

May we soon again rally around this ship, which is hand in (fighting) glove with each flight and co-responsible for the groups' success.

Put 'er there, gang—you've got what it takes! . . . so here's to Ten, a fighting gang of men.

> —GROUP COMMANDER R. K. GAINES, commanding Air Group, *Enterprise*, to the TEN squadrons, on November 17th, 1942

This letter was written by Lt. John Leppla on the night of Oct. 25—the eve of Santa Cruz—to be forwarded to his mother if he did not survive the action.

Somewhere in the Southwest Pacific
October 25, 1942

Dear Mother,

This letter will not be mailed unless I fail to return from an anticipated mission. Within the next three hours we expect a large scale battle against an enemy superior in numbers and equipment. There can be no alternative for either side. The battle must be decisive. I hope I can do my part well before I go. I hope there will be no undue sorrow with my passing. Live for the living. We who are gone must be considered the price of freedom. Some must die so that others may live. I am glad to be able to give my life in the hope that someday men will learn to stop fighting and live together peaceably.

Good-bye,

John

(John Leppla did not return from this action. This letter is reprinted by permission of his Mother. The will and personal messages have been deleted.)

LIST OF ILLUSTRATIONS

THE GRIM REAPERS

Chapter 1

FIRE TEST

IT WAS the hour before dawn. Two great American aircraft carriers, the *Lexington* and *Yorktown,* rolled gently as they pushed massive hulls through the long, lazy swells of the southwest Pacific. Beyond the horizon, far outside visual range, a great fleet of Japanese warships—several carriers, a few battleships, some cruisers and an array of destroyers —stretched in an arc from the northwest around to the east of the small American task force they sought to destroy. The Japanese objective was to wipe out this force and thus clear the way for a sea-borne invasion of Port Moresby.

The American carriers traveled slowly. The big *Yorktown,* flying Rear Admiral Frank Fletcher's flag, had the *Neosho—* a squat fleet tanker affectionately known as the Fat Lady— lying nearby and was drinking in thousands of gallons of fuel oil to satiate her boilers, and stores of aviation gasoline for her brood of war birds. Connecting hoses hung suspended above the sea as the two vessels steamed along. The *Yorktown* was last of the fleet to replenish her fuel supplies; her accompanying vessels had quenched their thirst earlier.

Keen-eyed lookouts on the flagship could scarcely distinguish the dark smudge off her port beam that was the *Lexington.* Off to starboard other, dimmer smudges indicated the screening ships, none of which showed the faintest gleam of light. Aboard, everyone slept except the watch on duty.

The *Lexington* drew away imperceptibly, her mighty turbines building up speed for launching the dawn scouts. Patrol fighters were already preparing to be sent aloft as a

19

protecting umbrella against possible enemy surprise attack.

Suddenly gongs clanged and bugles sounded. Booming over the loudspeaker systems, they penetrated to every part of the assembled vessels, calling all hands to "stations." Sailors learn early not to linger or to grouse when they are summarily roused from slumber. Officers and men, sound asleep a moment before the call, tumbled from their bunks, dressed hastily, hurried through the long passageways and clambered up and down steel gangways to their posts. They followed, almost mechanically, a routine many times rehearsed.

Whether this was the usual morning "stand-to," practiced daily in wartime, or the real thing, they couldn't tell, although they were well aware that their craft was cruising in waters near to enemy warships. Would the first rays of the early sun bring hostile planes winging in to deliver bomb and torpedo visiting cards? Would the dawn sky disclose the silhouettes of enemy warships, or would a lurking submarine be lying in wait?

Members of the air squadrons, complete in flying kit, helmets, goggles, and carrying their flight navigation boards, reported to the ready rooms. On deck, powerful aero engines coughed and roared as mechanics warmed up the power plants. Hot coffee made the rounds as the pilots, bringing their own data up to the minute, copied last-minute information from the big blackboard. They had jotted down air velocity at each thousand feet of altitude, the direction, intended course and speed of their carrier during the next few hours, information on weather and the location of the reference point—that position of latitude and longitude from which they and the carrier would read all distances and compass bearings throughout the morning. Naturally, no radio messages could be sent by either that might give the position of the carriers.

The signalmen on the bridge of the *Yorktown* watched the

dim shape of the now speeding *Lexington* through their 'scopes and carefully noted each streak of flame from the exhausts as the *Lex's* planes raced along the flight deck to the extreme bow, took to the air, circled and, fanning outward like the spokes of a wheel, disappeared to scan the ocean for hostile ships. In quiet voices the signalmen numbered the planes launched and soon reported twenty SBDs (scout dive bombers) and eight VFs (fighter planes) in flight. The fleet's tension did not lessen until an hour or more after the planes had taken off. There was no immediate danger of attack now, for the scouts would have spotted and reported the enemy if he were near.

Once more the sailors settled down to their shipboard duties. On deck the aircraft crews (to whom goes credit for keeping the planes well tuned and groomed) made use of the brightening sky to work on their charges. The *Yorktown's* airmen eased out of their flight clothes. Some prepared for breakfast, others continued to shoot the breeze, which is Navy lingo for idle palaver. Standing with the breeze shooters was Lieutenant Commander James H. Flatley, executive officer of the *Yorktown's* fighter squadron, VF-42.

Out of Green Bay, Wisconsin, Jim had graduated from the Naval Academy at Annapolis in 1929. After serving as a deck officer, he had entered the Naval Air Station at Pensacola, Florida, in 1930 to become a flier. With the exception of short foreign duty in the Mediterranean as senior flier aboard the cruiser *Omaha,* when she was guarding American interests during the Spanish Civil War, and another spell as instructor at Pensacola, he had been with squadrons aboard various flat-tops, the last of which was the *Lexington.* He had come on duty aboard the *Yorktown* only recently.

A Marine orderly entered the ready room and told Flatley that Captain Elliott Buckmaster requested him to report at the captain's quarters. Jim climbed the steel ladder to the bridge and entered the emergency cabin. Captain Buckmaster received him with a friendly nod, invited him to sit down, and handed Flatley the copy of a signal just now recorded. As Jim read it, a wide grin spread over his face. It was an order for him to take the first available transportation to the west coast, where he was to form and command a new fighter squadron, VF-10. It was a first-class assignment.

The captain congratulated him, and suggested he had better pack quickly, get some breakfast and transfer to the *Neosho,* which would cast off soon and take him at least part way home.

Jim's face fell at this advice. Like everyone else aboard, he was sure that the ship would be engaged in battle soon and he had no intention of leaving at this stage. Reflecting a few moments, he made his request quietly: "Captain, we are expecting a big battle. I would like to be allowed to remain and see it through. I could pick up transportation after it's over. Surely you could use another pilot here."

It was a sensible appeal. Captain Buckmaster considered it silently and responded at last: "There may be a way. Let me have an hour to work it out. But remember, I can't promise anything."

Flatley thanked him and took his leave. Back in the ready room he found two members of the scouting squadron, Lieutenant Stanley Vejtasa and Lieutenant Fritz Faulkner. Mightily excited, they informed him that they had just been ordered to transfer to the *Neosho* and report to the San Diego Naval Air Station, where they would become fighter pilots in VF-10. Their belongings already rested on the *Neosho's* deck, and they intended to follow after breakfast.

When Faulkner and Vejtasa heard that Flatley was to be their new skipper and had requested to stay aboard for the battle, they insisted on remaining, too. Surely, Vejtasa argued, two experienced fliers shouldn't be refused a chance to get a crack at the Japs.

Laughing, Jim had to promise that he would make a similar request for them if his were granted. He went below for bacon and eggs then, but found the food difficult to swallow. Around him were his squadron mates, a gay and cheerful bunch. They heaped congratulations upon him because he was headed home, and they joked together as if they had no cares at all. Jim knew he would miss them. Watching the clock, he forced himself to eat. An hour later he mounted the familiar steel steps to the captain's quarters. Buckmaster greeted Jim with one of his rare smiles.

"I have made arrangements for you to stay with us, and I am glad to have you aboard," he said.

Jim put in quickly: "Lieutenants Vejtasa and Faulkner also ask permission to see this thing through with the ship, sir."

"Well, all right. I see no reason why not, now that you're remaining, because they can't do much back there until you arrive."

Overjoyed, Jim hurried below to pass on the good word. The two scout pilots were waiting for him anxiously at the foot of the ladder. They waited only to catch his affirmative nod before they scrambled out on the deck to have their baggage brought back.

Flatley went on below and busied himself unpacking his heavy flight clothing and other uniforms, hanging them on their accustomed hooks. The family pictures went back to their old place on his desk. Things were shipshape again.

Back in the wardroom, Jim found most of his squadron assembled, glad that he was staying. He felt deeply all their warmth and sincerity, their true comradeship. For a moment, when he had thought of his wife and children, he wondered if he shouldn't have taken the opportunity to go home, but inside he knew it was right for him to stay. That's what he had been trained for, these long years.

Aboard the *Lexington* were three other men who, unwitting, were to become part of Flatley's VF-10. One was Lieutenant Dave Pollock, an old-time flier. Now, to his chagrin, he found himself on duty as assistant air officer to Commander Herbert Duckworth. Pollock had been a contented member of Scouting 2 when Commander Duckworth became air officer in the summer of 1941 and chose him for Air Plot. (Air Plot is that department aboard a carrier where all air information is collected and from which fighter and attack planes are directed.) But a flier in a non-flying job is always an unhappy man, particularly in wartime.

The other two men, Lieutenant John Leppla and Lieutenant Bobby Edwards, members of Lieutenant Commander Bob Dixon's Scouting 2, were out searching for Japanese warships and did not return until nearly ten o'clock that morning. They had no inkling they were to be switched to another squadron, and before the transfer could take place, they had a job to do on Japanese warships and aircraft.

The *Neosho*, her mission completed, uncoupled hoses and cast off. Her skipper, waving good luck, rang below for increased speed, ordered hard right helm and swung away for home, escorted by the destroyer *Sims*.

"Donald Duck," the carrier's loudspeaker system (so-called because of the peculiar clack-clack sound made by the announcer's voice), proclaimed that the "smoking lamp is on," thus lifting the ban which had prohibited all smoking during the refueling process. While the *Neosho* wove through the screening ships, Rear Admiral Fletcher ordered more speed for the fleet. The task force quickened its pace; it was ready for action.

To relieve the *Lex's* air group, the *Yorktown* now launched her scouts, and VF-42 fighter pilots took up their Wildcats for protective combat patrol.

About 10:30 A.M., Jim Flatley, flying above an overcast which lowered visibility to 5000 feet, radioed that he had spotted a Kawanishi, a four-engined Japanese flying boat used as a long-range, armed-patrol plane. The enemy expended these big aircraft freely in order to discover the whereabouts of Allied warships. Jim asked his ship to watch for the Jap and announced he was going after the enemy craft. A moment later the fleet saw the Kawanishi breaking through the clouds, burning fiercely, streaking straight downward. Blazing wreckage smashed into the sea and heavy black smoke marked the funeral pyre—in true Japanese style.

Although this disposed of the snooper, its presence indicated that the enemy fleet had been notified of our location. "Where are the Japs?" we wanted to know. "Are their carriers within range? Will they attack?" We intensified our search.

Darkness closed down and the last scout returned. Not one Jap vessel had been spotted within several hundred miles. The Kawanishi, it must be assumed, had flown from one of the several bases established by the enemy in the Solomon Island group to the north.

Before nightfall, a radio message from General Douglas MacArthur's headquarters in Australia notified the force that a hostile fleet of two carriers, five cruisers and ten destroyers had been seen late that afternoon by an Army long-range patrol plane. This fleet had passed through the northern Solomons, heading south at twenty knots. It was plain that the enemy ships, if they continued on their course at this speed, would reach the northern shore of Misima at sunrise. Rapid calculation showed that a fast run north during the night would bring our ships within air range by dawn.

The crew stood to "stations" for the sunset hour, a most dangerous period at sea. As the men went below after the order to "secure" had been given, the whole fleet changed course. Hour after hour the vessels drove northward, and as morning dawned they were standing off to the southeast of Rossel Island.

The *Yorktown's* scouts, already aloft except for a few held on deck in reserve, were to be armed with bombs to accompany the attack group as dive bombers, as were most of the *Lexington's* Scouting 2, including Leppla and Edwards. Flatley was assigned to lead a section of Wildcats to protect the *Yorktown's* torpedo planes.

Since it was expected that the scouts would take more than an hour to reach the enemy, the fliers ate breakfast, then trooped to the ready rooms for last-minute corrections. They were prepared for imminent battle.

At 8:10 A.M. came the first scout radio report. A Japanese fleet of one carrier, five cruisers and ten destroyers had been sighted about fifty miles north of Misima, or about two hundred miles from the American ships. Air crews rushed to their stations, the carriers, whose speed had been built up to give maximum assistance in the take-off of the heavily laden torpedo planes and dive bombers, turned into the wind and the planes sped toward an enemy who unsuspectingly continued his southward course. In their approach, our planes closed the range by another twenty miles, thus slightly shortening the distance.

The weather was excellent and our squadron commanders had no difficulty locating the ships. Both carriers' squadrons massed for the assault, and before the enemy had a chance to realize it, the American planes were upon them. Down screamed the dive bombers from 15,000 feet in almost vertical dives, closely followed by low-flying torpedo planes, to deliver their "pickles." Too late, the Jap carrier turned frantically into the wind to launch its planes. Our dive bombers loosed their 1000-pounders for the plunge, aiming projectiles which would penetrate through decks and explode deep inside the hull.

One of the first bomber pilots to swoop down was Leppla.

As he aimed his plane at the target far below, his radioman, D. K. Liska, tensed in the rear seat with free machine gun ready. Having had too short a warning, and failing to get high enough for interception, a few Zeros attempted to run interference by diving with the Americans, shooting at whatever plane came into their sights. Two of them overtook Leppla while he was in his slowed-down dive, with air brakes extended. Liska drew a bead on the nearest one and shot him down. The second flashed past and began to shoot at the American bomber in front. Leppla closed up, pouring slugs from his pair of fixed wing machine guns into the Jap's fuselage. The Zero took fire and fell out of control.

This interference caused Leppla to miss the carrier by a few feet with his 500-pounder, but he still had a 100-pounder under each wing. Pulling out of his dive, he saw another Zero on his tail, turned steeply and shot it out of the air, then climbed, selected a cruiser and let her have it. From his grandstand position in the rear, Liska saw at least one of the 100-pounders smash on the deck and explode.

The two pilots, their mission completed, started out for home. Halfway across the one hundred and eighty miles of ocean between them and their base, they spotted a Jap two-seater float fighter plane, chased it and, in a duel over the Louisiade Archipelago, sent it flaming to the bottom. Only then, having neither ammunition nor gas to spare, they made for the *Lexington*.

Flatley, at about 5000 feet above the *Yorktown's* torpedo squadron (headed by Lieutenant Commander Joe Taylor), saw the heavy-laden, slow-flying planes approach the Jap carrier at only fifty feet above the sea. Two Zeros, flying in from nowhere, suddenly attacked the squadron, whose skipper spotted them and radioed for assistance. Flatley and his wing mate, Lieutenant John Baker, dived and took on the enemy pair. Flatley lined a Zero in his sights, pressed the firing button and watched his tracers enter the Jap's fuselage, perforating it.

Speaking of it later, Jim reported: "I was astonished at the way the stream of .50-caliber slugs from my four guns chopped the Jap plane into shreds. But even more awe-inspiring was the manner in which the heavy bullets threw up a great shower of water as they splashed into the sea below and in front of me. Never before had I fired all four guns at once into the water. Before the war, while training, we economized and never fired more than two at a time.

"As I recovered and made ready to take a shot at another Zero, I had the feeling of having an instrument of tremendous destructive ability in my hands. From that moment, the Wildcat meant a good deal to me, because I'd seen what it could accomplish."

Vejtasa and Faulkner, high up with the *Yorktown* dive bombers, peeled off at 15,000 feet, sending their heavy bombs into the vitals of the stricken carrier. They saw the big vessel literally torn to pieces before their eyes and disappear from sight within a few minutes.

As the carriers steamed away with their victorious flock, they got a radio message from the *Neosho*. She and the destroyer *Sims* had been attacked by enemy planes. The *Sims* sank almost at once, after a square hit on her narrow fantail. Later, the radio reported that the *Neosho* was wallowing low in the water, her engines and boilers smashed, her battered hull kept afloat only by her still unbroken empty gas tanks.

The attacking aircraft had obviously been seeking bigger game. They had passed on high without taking notice at first, and the leading squadrons were over before the dive bombers dropped down to aim their bombs. Still later that morning other enemy squadrons, returning from early flights, again attacked the already half-sunken tanker. She drifted helplessly for several days before one of our destroyers found her, took off her survivors and wounded, then sent the little ship to the bottom.

Vejtasa and Faulkner took the news of the *Neosho's* sinking in silence. They realized their narrow escape.

"Battle stations" sounded again just before dark. Pilots hurried to the ready rooms and mechanics started the motors. "Donald Duck" quacked that enemy planes were in the vicinity.

Flatley, ordered to take five other VFs and climb to find the enemy ships, ran to his plane and saw Lieutenant E. Scott McCusky already in the cockpit, a hopeful look on his face. Mac was in the doghouse that day. (Later, he would make headlines by shooting down two planes the following day and five more in the Midway action.) He had been grounded by his skipper for violating sound combat procedure three days previously during an attack on Tulagi Harbor, where he had broken formation to go after some Japs. Now he was not allowed upstairs.

"I motioned him out," Flatley relates. "Crestfallen, and with a voice fairly dripping disappointment, he begged: 'Mr. Flatley, won't you give me a plane?'

"As much as I wanted to take him, I knew that to relax discipline at this point would ruin the whole idea behind punishment, so I had to shake my head.

"He climbed out reluctantly and I hopped aboard, revved up the engine and the deck plane handlers led my ship to the starting line. Soon I was racing along the deck into the air."

With a roar, all the Wildcats gathered speed and took off, Flatley and Lieutenant John Baker, his wing man, leading as they climbed. Visibility was bad. Rain squalls hid everything up to more than 2000 feet, where the fliers broke into the clear. Even there it was not very bright because the sun was down; only its reflection came over the distant horizon.

"As we climbed," Flatley recalls, "the quiet, reassuring voice of Lieutenant 'Red' Gill, fighter director of the *Lex*, who had been my roommate when I was aboard her, came over the radio. 'Hello, Jim, old boy. Glad to have you with me again. I want you to look for a bunch of Jap machines reported out on our starboard beam.'

"Climbing to the point directed, I heard Paul Ramsey, skipper of Fighting 2, communicate with his wing man, Ensign George Markham, on the intercom. 'What are we looking for?' I asked, cutting in.

"Paul's voice came back with a 'Hi, Jimmy! We're working on some Zeros.' Just then I saw some big dull blobs dropping through the rain—burning Jap planes, plummeting to the tune of the *Lexington's* fighter guns.

"We were flying at 2000 feet, just on top of the rain clouds, when I noted the shadows of three planes pass below me at high speed. Art Wollen, leader of the last section of my six Wildcats, saw them too. He and Ensign Knox broke formation and dived to attack. They chased the Japs about sixty miles and shot down two of them. The third brought down Art's wing man by perforating his motor with bullet holes, forcing him to land in the water about a hundred miles out.

"I led the three remaining Wildcats ahead into the squall until we broke into a small clear patch where several Jap bombers were scurrying into the safety of the thick weather. They were a glossy olive drab, with a bright red band around the fuselage. I selected one almost down on the sea and dove at him, followed by the rest of my section. When the Nip's rear gunner opened with his 20-mm. cannon, the heavy rain magnified the size of each muzzle flash many times, accentuating it so that the discharge much resembled the shooting of a 75-mm. gun.

"He fired a few rounds as I approached, and just when I was about to open fire there was a big, blinding glare slightly below and astern of the enemy machine. He had

released some kind of gimcrack, maybe an explosive magnesium flare, like the Nazis use sometimes to discourage a
fighter closing in from astern. He let go a few more of these
fireworks. By then I was in close enough to let him have it.
Slanting downward, my four .50s ripped into him. The sea
was now only a few feet below, but I could not see it for the
rain. I hauled back on the stick and thought my wing tip
skimmed the water. I looked around but the Jap had disappeared.

"As I zoomed back out of the line of fire of the Wildcats
following me, I turned and saw Lieut. MacComber set fire to
a Jap dive bomber. This Kogekiki exploded wildly, scattering
blazing bits over a wide area. It was a wonderful display
of pyrotechnics.

"I ordered a rendezvous low on the water, above the
widening oil slick which was all that remained of the Nip.
I wanted to be sure that the rest of the section did not get
separated in this weather. We could see only a few yards
in the rain, by this time. It was practically dark.

"We gathered and headed off in the general direction
taken by Art Wollen and his wing man when they broke
away in pursuit of the enemy, a course away from the carrier. But we didn't see anything for about twenty-five miles,
and couldn't raise the carrier over the radio, so I decided
to turn back.

"I formed Lieutenant John Baker in left echelon, with the
other pair in right, kept my radio on voice frequency and
asked Baker to lead us back to the Yorktown.

"It isn't exactly easy to keep track of your plane's position
while flying and fighting at low visibility, especially when
your roost is streaking ahead at top speed, making violent
course changes all the time. We had flown various courses
in the past hour, seeing nothing except rain and the blank
surface of the sea, now darkness was all around us. Dead
reckoning, keeping track of position by noting down all com-

pass courses flown, allowing for wind drift, computing speed
—all those things were not much help.

"But Baker, a first-class airman, led us right through the
blackness to the carrier. We made our approach, switched
on our lights and gave the recognition signal. Then we broke
formation and formed into the landing circle. At this point,
we were ordered to shut off our running lights. We did it,
although we knew it was going to be hard to keep track of
each other in the night. After several minutes, orders were
reissued to commence landing.

"After I'd set down my Wildcat, I stood on the deck
counting noses as the others came in. Just then there was a
disturbance above us in the dark. Nine strange planes, all
showing lights, passed slowly to starboard, strung out for a
landing. They were Japs!

"Far off to port a destroyer illuminated the first plane with
its searchlight and immediately erupted flame as every gun
opened fire. Several other ships followed suit. For a few
minutes the sky was a mass of bursting shells and streams
of tracer bullets.

"Astounded by this welcome, the enemy planes doused
their lights and the survivors disappeared to the west.
Shortly afterward, we learned that a big force of hostile warships was just thirty miles away, hidden by the same bad
weather enveloping our vessels. Baker, after leading us back,
was still aloft when the Japs got lost in the murk and mis-
took our fleet for theirs. The lookouts told me that Baker
chased them. Commander Oscar Peterson, in charge of Air
Plot, immediately broke radio silence to contact Baker and
tell him to return to the ship. John answered that he had
lost his bearings and wasn't sure which way to turn to get
back.

"For the next two hours we played one of those tragic
dramas between lost plane and mother ship. John's voice
came over the intercom from somewhere out in the storm,

These are the Reapers: Left to right, front row — Leder, Feightner, Coalson, Kona, Flatley, Kain, Gaskill, Wickendoll, Eckhardt, Porter. Center row — McClaugherty, Voris, Pollock, Taber, Boydston, Harmon, Ruehlow, Donahaugh, Gordon, Billo, Slagel, Kanzie, Hedrick, Faulkner, Vejtasa, Long. Back row — Kilpatrick, Reiserer, Whitte, Murphy, Harris, Schonk, Reding, Heinston, Boren. (*Chicago Tribune Photo*)

Lieutenant Commander James H. Flatley in the cockpit of the Wildcat plane in which he led the Grim Reapers. (*Chicago Tribune Photo*)

Lieutenant John A. Leppla, the Reaper who shot down seven Japanese Zero fighters in the Battle of the Coral Sea. Leppla was listed as missing in the Battle of Santa Cruz, on October 26th, 1942.
(*Press Association Photo*)

asking for directions back to the carrier. We worked continually trying to guide him aboard. Only a little while before his radio had led us unerringly home through the same storm; now, for some reason, it had gone haywire. We tried over and over, without any luck, to tune our radio to his voice frequency so we could give him a compass course, but maybe his compass wasn't working properly, or his radio was out. His squadron mates, and other men off duty, stood around listening to the voice of the fighter director coaching him back, and John's cheerful voice answering from time to time.

"I began to watch the clock. As time ticked off, I knew his fuel was running low and that he'd have to crash-land soon. I never felt so helpless. Everything possible was being done, but it was pretty bad to stand there inactive. John Baker was probably the only cheerful man in the whole assembled fleet. He never once appeared discouraged.

"He must have flown out of the bad weather area, finally, because he reported that he could see what appeared to be a small island and was going to land. Commander Peterson wished him good luck. And Baker's voice came back, confident and strong, 'Good luck to you, sir.'

"That was more than fifteen months ago. He's still missing.

"We should have been glad to chalk up a Jap carrier, a cruiser and twenty-three planes to our credit, but we were a sad bunch that night. The day's victory was a washout now, for us, and we were dog-tired besides.

"We might have felt worse if it hadn't been for Commander Dixie Kiefer, the *Yorktown's* executive officer. He seemed to be everywhere at once, in spite of the numerous jobs assigned to the 'exec' of a carrier. He found time to call in on the fliers, sensing our need for some cheering up, for someone to take our mind off Baker, Knox and six other boys lost during the day's action. His reassuring manner and priceless ability to say the right thing, always, helped tremen-

dously. He left the ready room, after a heartening word to
every one of us, and we went off to bed, feeling much better.

"But there wasn't any sleep for Dixie that night. He moved
about the ship, dropping in on every department from the
fire rooms to the sky lookouts, making sure his men were
comfortable and restoring confidence to officers and enlisted
men alike. Captain Buckmaster was confident, too, and Commander Murr Arnold, our air officer, told us we would fight
the Japs to a standstill next day. He advised us all to get as
much sleep as possible.

"I found 'Swede' Vejtasa in my room and he told me of
the *Neosho's* sinking. I hadn't heard this sad news. During
the first hectic months of the war, the *Neosho* had ser-
viced the *Lex* and the *Yorktown* many times while I was
aboard one or the other and we had all developed an affec-
tion for her. I got to know several of her officers and men
during the hours she had been with us. We had escaped their
fate by a narrow margin; we felt that we had a lot to be
thankful for that day."

Next morning, May 8, was bright and clear. The enemy
fleet lay somewhere near by; it was only a matter of finding,
fixing and fighting it.

At 8 A.M., the voice of Ensign Smith, one of the *Lexington's* SPD-2 scouts, reported contact with a powerful enemy
fleet—two carriers, three battleships, numerous cruisers and
destroyers—two hundred miles to the north. Smith's squadron leader, Lieutenant Commander Bob Dixon, flying over
the enemy, amplified the report.

Just before the attack group was launched, the skipper
of Fighting 42 lifted the penalty on "Go get 'em" McCusky,
making him the happiest man aboard. Mac took off with his
squadron mates, Bill Leonard, 'Art Wollen and Ensign
Adams, to escort the *Yorktown's* bombers, and they were

intercepted by Zeros. Young McCusky celebrated by shooting down two of them.

How the American carrier pilots smashed through the screen of defending Zeros and attacked two Japanese carriers has since become history. The score sheet shows three 1000-pound bombs and five torpedo hits on one flat-top, and bomb and torpedo hits on the second. One carrier was definitely destroyed and the second severely damaged. The last fliers to leave reported her ablaze, listing badly.

It was during this attack that Ensign Joseph ("Jo Jo") Powers sacrificed himself in his determination to lay a heavy bomb on the deck of the Jap carrier. For this the Navy posthumously awarded him the Congressional Medal of Honor, which went to his proud parents.

At 11:14 A.M., 103 Japanese naval aircraft came over and began one of the war's most ferocious air assaults. Out of the sun the dive bombers struck, and from almost sea level, all around the circle, swooped the torpedo planes. Warships blazed at them from all sides with hundreds of guns, while a small brood of Wildcats and slow-flying scout planes—eight of each type—engaged them in an air combat which set a new high for percentage of planes destroyed in one short battle. When the shooting ended sixteen minutes later, the ship's gunners had bagged nineteen and the fliers forty-four enemy planes.

This day's action tested Lieutenant Vejtasa effectually and raised him without question to the ranks of our greatest airmen. Four days previously, with the *Yorktown's* SBD-5, he had shuttled back and forth across Guadalcanal, carrying bombs, and secured a direct hit on a Jap vessel. The day before, flying his Douglass Dauntless, he had participated in the dive-bombing of the Japanese carrier that was sunk by the combined air groups of the *Yorktown* and *Lex*. On this day, he and five squadron mates took off from the *Yorktown*

in their Dauntless scout bombers, without bombs. Part of the
protective screen, they were sent out to intercept low-flying
enemy torpedo planes.

The Dauntless, designed as a dive bomber and scout,
has neither the fire power nor the speed of a fighter, even
when it is not carrying bombs. It is more than a hundred
miles per hour slower than a fighter. Its armament consists
of only two fixed .50-caliber machine guns in the wing
(they shoot forward and are aimed by pointing the plane at
the target) and a free light machine gun mounted in the
rear seat to enable the radio operator ensconced there to fire
it. This gun can be fired on a slant over either wing, down
on either side, outward on both flanks, or upward and to
the rear past the tail fin.

Similar types of Japanese aircraft are looked upon by our
fighter pilots as duck soup and whole flights of them are
frequently annihilated when caught without Zero escorts.
In the absence of enemy fighters, our Dauntless can be used
against torpedo planes, which are loaded with heavy "fish"
whose 2000-pound weight cuts the ship's performance, and
thus the Dauntless can outspeed and outfly them.

On this particular morning, all but a group of Wildcats
were out escorting our dive bombers and torpedo planes in
their attack on the enemy; consequently Admiral Fletcher
had no other choice but to employ his few Wildcats at high
altitude to intercept the Jap dive bombers, and to send his
few remaining Dauntless pilots off to deal with the Jap torpedo planes.

Vejtasa's six-plane section was cruising at 11:14 o'clock,
waiting for the approach of the Japs, when twelve Zeros
attacked. The Japs had the advantage of diving out of the
sun and weren't seen until they were almost within shooting
range. It was an overhead attack, and in their first blitz they
shot down two of the Dauntless scouts. The other four had
broken formation in taking evasive action to escape.

Swede has since been quoted: "I found myself all alone with seven or eight Zeros above, nipping in and out, attacking from all sides. I've never felt so alone in my life."

Realizing that his life depended upon keeping cool, Swede shouted over the intercom to his radioman: "Son, we're in for a scrap. Keep your head and conserve your ammunition. Don't let the Japs catch you with an empty gun. I'll take care of the rest."

(It should be explained that the rear gun is charged with ammunition in magazines. As the gunner uses up each magazine, he has to loosen the old one and replace it with a filled can. This means a delay of a few seconds. Approaching warily and remaining out of range, in the hope that the gunner will begin shooting and continue for the six or so seconds it takes for the magazine to empty, the enemy planes then attempt to dive in while he is caught changing.)

Swede's radioman answered: "Aye, aye, sir! You can depend on me."

During this exchange, the Zeros deployed for the kill. Some stationed themselves on either beam, others drew ahead. The Zeros on the beam began to turn in and dive. These attacks were feints to occupy Swede and enable the others to make a run from ahead to shoot down the Dauntless. But the boy from Circle, Montana, could not be fooled so easily. He watched cautiously and kept track of every Jap; he fought with a frigid kind of calm. As each Zero feinted from the side, he resorted to his ailerons to dip his wing, allowing his rear gunner a shot with the free machine gun. At the same time, he dropped his nose to line up the Jap coming in from below and ahead, and squirted him with shots from his fixed bow guns.

The radio operator, doubling as rear gunner, did a fine job of conserving ammunition and never once let himself be caught with an empty magazine. The Japs learned to respect that free gun and kept at extreme range. Their plan wasn't coming off so well; pilot and gunner were obviously not distracted.

This gruesome game went on for twenty-four minutes, a lifetime in the air, in which a distance of perhaps a hundred miles was covered. Three times Swede's fixed guns set a Zero on fire and sent it crashing into the sea. The others finally drew off and climbed into a cloud. They had met their master in aerial combat tactics.

Finding the air clear of enemy planes, Swede was able to breathe again, but he kept vigilant eyes on the lookout, meanwhile congratulating his rear gunner on a masterly piece of work.

Weeks later, seated in the Navy Department in Washington, Swede was interviewed by senior naval officers on this engagement. Upon completing his story, he was asked: "And then what did you do, Vejtasa?"

His answer bowled them over. "Well, sir, I went back to my position off the port bow of the *Yorktown* and continued my patrol until ordered to return aboard."

This quiet remark was perhaps the best indication of Swede's character.

For John Leppla, the battle opened as he cruised at an altitude of 5000 feet, several miles from the fleet, with imperturbable Liska at the free gun in the rear seat of the Dauntless. Abruptly enemy torpedo planes began to spill out of a cloud at almost his exact level, passing rapidly in full power glides toward the ships.

With several other *Lex* scouts, Leppla dived and opened fire. He had the satisfaction of seeing his first victim belch smoke, then flare up as the gas load caught fire. Before he could recover from his downhill run, he was attacked by a squadron of fast-flying Zeros. He turned, fired and drove off the leading Zeros. Others came up from astern and Liska went to work on them efficiently. More Zeros lanced in, shooting and pulling up for a new dive. Liska sent one down in flames. Momentarily the others drew off, and in the short respite Leppla noticed another member of his section, Lieutenant Hall, in serious trouble.

Hall had already downed two Kogekiki torpedo planes and two Zeros and, unknown to Leppla, had been wounded in both feet by Japanese bullets. (Hall was later awarded the Congressional Medal of Honor for his heroic fight.) Two Zeros attacked Hall's damaged plane from astern. Leppla, about a thousand feet above, broke off action with the planes attacking him and dived to assist Hall. The Japs had been so intent upon making a kill that Leppla's intrusion was completely unexpected. Before his first target had a chance to dodge, John sent it careening into the sea. The second machine banked sharply and fled from the terror.

But the boys were still not out of the woods. One of their fixed nose guns had been shot out by enemy bullets and the other was out of ammunition. Limping back to the *Lex,* they were again attacked by two Zeros. They fought them off with the rear gun. The unruffled Liska fired the last of his ammunition with superb accuracy and the two Japs withdrew, one with a smoking engine.

When they finally landed on the carrier, their Dauntless was fairly riddled with bullets and explosives from 20-mm. cannon shell. The ship's right side was torn to shreds with machine-gun bullets. Nonchalantly, Leppla asked to be given another plane to continue his patrol, all the while picking spent shell fragments from his flying suit. Liska, as usual, "had nothing to say to no one." He was a fighting, not a talking, man.

Jim Flatley, whose skipper had elected to lead the escorting fighters of VF-42, was aboard the *Yorktown* on defensive patrol. He and some other VF-42 fighters were kept back on deck until the last minute to guarantee that they would begin the action with full fuel tanks and a maximum of ammunition.

Word came at 11:05 A.M. that a large force of hostile dive bombers and torpedo planes was approaching. The *Yorktown* swung into the wind and the Wildcats, led by Jim, were launched. As they climbed for altitude in a full-throttle steep climb, they heard Paul Ramsey, skipper of the *Lex's* Fighting 2, report from 12,000 feet that thirty-six hostile aircraft were passing about four thousand feet above him. They were the first attack wave of eighteen dive bombers and eighteen Zeros.

As Flatley tells it: "We discovered the Japs' presence when we had reached only 8000 feet, and this was followed immediately by a report from scouts flying in the anti-torpedo plane screen that they were intercepting Japs at 5000 feet, or a couple of miles closer to the fleet. So we swung around to look for the enemy below us.

"As we turned, I spotted a flight of Zeros swooping on our scouts below. Giving the tallyho to my accompanying VFs, I nosed over and rushed in for the Zeros.

"There is one thing a Wildcat can do better than a Zero, and that's dive. Coming down faster than the Zeros, we caught them unawares. The Nip fighters, too eager to get at the easy-mark SBDs, hadn't noticed our approach until our tracers began to zip past them as we opened fire. The enemy scattered and our Wildcats were soon split up in individual dogfights over a wide area.

"I picked out a Zero who tried to pull away from a climb in order to return to the fight. With a thousand feet of altitude on him, I was able to slant down. The pickup from this downhill, full-power glide brought me into the line of fire. At four hundred yards, I opened with a ranging burst, released the firing button when I was within two hundred yards, and then let him have another three-second burst. My four .50s firing together shredded that Zero and left a falling mass of burning debris where the plane had been.

"I went into a climb to look for the other pilots in my group, but they were nowhere about. In the melee, they had drawn away in duels with other Zeros. Looking around, I spotted three cruising Zeros slightly below. I tipped over and swept down on them. Just as I was about to open fire on one, he turned quickly toward me and pulled back in a steep climbing turn. Evidently he had been warned by one of the others.

"Then I made a serious error. Intent on getting him, I hauled my Wildcat around sharply and pulled my nose up out of the dive. Executing this violent turn and about-face at the excessive speed of my dive was more than I could take and I blacked out. I was unconscious for maybe three seconds. When I was able to see again, my Wildcat was in an almost vertical climb, passing the Zero so closely that we were wing tip to wing tip. The Jap pilot was now attempting to draw in behind on my quarter for a shot.

"In the brief moment we were abeam of each other, I saw the Jap with a confident smirk on his yellow face, sure he had me. I remember being impressed by the excellent paint job on his machine, which was finished in light brown with a broad black stripe from the bottom of the windshield along the cowling to the nose. This was my first close-up of a Mitsubishi Zero and I was struck with its businesslike appearance, its smooth exterior.

"By that time I had a grip on myself again. It was about time. I was beginning to lose speed from climbing too steeply. My air-speed indicator registered only 110 knots, and I knew that I had to get out of this climb fast before the engine stalled, or the Jap would be sieving my Grumman with his 20-mm. cannon shells and the bullets from his front pair of 7.7 machine guns. Although the range was point-blank, the Jap still had to get his nose around a bit more to line me up in his sights. He was still flying almost parallel to my course, but in a moment he would have dropped back enough to turn in toward me.

"We were within a hair's breadth when I hauled back on the stick, risking a collision. My plane answered the stabilizer smoothly and looped right over the Zero. Still on my back, and above the first Zero, I saw a second one coming up from below. This forced me to continue the loop until I came over into a dive and picked up speed. I flattened out low down, twisting to evade their fire. When I looked for them again, the Japs had gone."

Faulkner, the fourth candidate for VF-10, had toted his bomb and sent it, along with more tokens of the same variety from other *Yorktown* dive bombers, into a Jap carrier. These bombers had little trouble from Jap planes because they had maintained formation and stayed under the protecting wing of their fighter escort.

Dave Pollock, fifth of the VF-10 sextette, was aboard the *Lexington,* in the unenviable position of a grounded bird. As assistant air officer, he had to stand on the bridge of his carrier, a pilot with his wings tied, forced to watch enemy aircraft dive and aim bombs at him without being able to do anything about it. To watch a dive bomber fly straight at your ship and see its sleek black bomb abandon the rack to plummet in your direction is never an enjoyable experience. On a ship there is no foxhole to duck into, nowhere to run.

One after the other, five Jap torpedoes thudded into the port side of the gallant *Lexington,* each burst sending a huge waterspout into the air—columns of solid sea weighing several tons. Violent concussions went through the brave old ship and shook her from stem to stern. Mortally wounded, she fought valiantly until the fires within her hull forced her to succumb.

Pollock counted nineteen enemy aircraft downed by the assembled warships and saw others set afire by the guns of the protecting fighter screen. Before nightfall he was transferred to a rescuing warship, along with Leppla, Bobby Edwards (then Leppla's executive officer, who had scored a bomb hit on one of the Jap carriers and was to be No. 6 in Jim Flatley's new group), and 92 per cent of the *Lexington's* crew. The survivors, from the ships to which they had been distributed, watched the *Lex* quiver, still upright, settle low and at last sink as three torpedoes from an American destroyer administered the *coup de grâce*.

The *Yorktown's* crew was busy examining the gap on her lacerated flight deck. A square hit had penetrated through the deck below and exploded in a storeroom. The heavy 14-inch bomb had been falling at about a 45-degree angle when it pierced the flight deck, and undoubtedly would have slanted through the open side but for the fact that it struck a steel beam which deflected it downward. Though it did no structural damage to the carrier, its blast had killed forty-two men.

When night closed in, the Japanese armada, licking its wounds, retired northward. Within five days, May 4–8 inclusive, the American carrier task force had sunk one Japanese carrier and damaged a second. Fourteen out of fifteen ships, ranging from cruisers to supply vessels, had been destroyed in Tulagi, and a heavy cruiser, along with a carrier, sent to the bottom off Misima.

The Japs had lost 216 planes—twelve squadrons, each consisting of eighteen machines—in the two carrier actions, besides having two shot out of the air and eight destroyed on the waters of Tulagi.

Our losses on May 8 had been twelve machines shot down and thirty, damaged during action, sunk aboard the *Lexington*. (The remainder of the *Lex's* aircraft had been saved by being flown aboard the *Yorktown*.) Our ship losses were the carrier *Lexington*, the destroyer *Sims* and the tanker *Neosho*.

The enemy's loss of life was extremely heavy. It has been

estimated that two thousand Japs went down with their vessels at Tulagi, where we nipped off one of the Japanese prongs. Off Misima, it was claimed that none of the two thousand to twenty-five hundred men on the carrier escaped destruction in the pasting she took from the nineteen bombs and eleven torpedoes which tore her to pieces. More were lost aboard the cruiser sunk in the same action.

It is difficult to estimate just how many Japs were killed on that eighth day of May, for apart from the hundred or so airmen who went down with their planes, we had no way of knowing how many hundreds were killed by the bombs and torpedoes which sent one carrier to the bottom and left another on fire.

It was the first defeat suffered by the Japanese in this war. It was also the first battle fought between aircraft-carrier battle forces, where the attack on ships had been delivered solely by planes. In all these actions, our forces had proved their quality to be superior to the enemy's, and that fact was to be borne out further by the engagements fought in 1942 and 1943.

Chapter 2

THE REAPERS ARE BORN

EIGHT DAYS after the Coral Sea engagement, several ships of Admiral Fletcher's carrier force were anchored at a small Pacific island. A hospital ship had taken several of the more serious battle casualties aboard, and the remaining wounded were comfortably bedded down in the hospital wards of two transports. The survivors of the *Lexington* had been distributed between the transports—that is, all except a few who had already been given other duties.

Jim Flatley, Swede Vejtasa and Fritz Faulkner had joined the *Lex's* survivors on the homeward journey. With them was Bob Dixon, skipper of Scouting 2, who had been a friend of Flatley's for years; the two shared a cabin on the trip. Most of Dixon's scouts were also aboard, including John Leppla and Bobby Edwards, who wanted Jim to take them in as members of his new squadron, provided they could get transfers. It has been the practice to break up battle-experienced squadrons in wartime and to distribute their skilled fliers among new and untried squadrons, so that the new outfits could get the benefit of the veterans' knowledge. But Leppla and Edwards were anxious to change over from scout bombers to fighters and they filled every requirement any squadron commander could possibly desire.

Flatley had followed the battles fought by Leppla through May 7 and 8 and he had noted the steadiness with which Edwards dropped his bombs on the Japs. He wanted the boys. Bob Dixon was so proud of his two lads that he would have done anything for them, but Navy permission for the

transfer could not be obtained until the transport reached
the United States.

Dave Pollock, too, felt there was nothing he wanted more
than to be taken into Jim's new outfit and return to the air
as a fighting pilot. Again Jim was delighted. He knew in-
stinctively that Dave would make a good fighter.

Meanwhile, "scuttlebutt" had it that Captain Ted Sherman, of the *Lexington*, was being promoted to rear admiral,
that Commander Duckworth would serve as his chief of
staff, and that Bob Dixon was slated to be air officer. Commander Duckworth had intended to take Pollock as a member of Rear Admiral Sherman's staff, but during the long
days and nights, while the slow transport churned across the
Pacific, he yielded, agreed to the shift, and gave his blessing
to Dave.

Thus the new fighter squadron, the first to be formed by
the Navy since December 7, 1941, began with three veteran
members each from the *Lexington* and *Yorktown* air groups.

The crowded transports arrived at a West Coast port late
one June day and it was 8:30 P.M. before the ships were
warped alongside the piers. Next morning Jim Flatley sat
down in the office assigned to him at the Naval Air Station
and began the task of organizing the new squadron. Vejtasa
and Faulkner reported, bringing with them Ensigns R. M.
Voris and James Dowden. These two youngsters had completed their training only recently and, with eight other ensigns, had been ordered to San Diego several days before to
report for VF-10, but these eight were then sent to sea on
temporary duty and were not expected back for another
week. Pollock, Leppla and Edwards had been granted a
month's leave, as had all other *Lex* men. That left only five of
the new squadron ready to begin work.

Ensign Roy Voris was a cheerful, twenty-three-year-old
from Santa Cruz, California. He stood six feet three inches
and weighed about two hundred and twenty-five pounds.

At Salinas Junior College he had been an all-around athlete —played tackle on the football team, threw the javelin and discus, and was also a good long-distance swimmer.

When Jim asked him what he had been doing since he left college, Voris reported: "I worked for a couple of years in Hollywood as a mortician's assistant in a top-notch undertaking parlor, but I left there fourteen months ago to fly for the Navy."

Jim remarked that he didn't think he could give Voris much more experience in embalming bodies, but he did hope to teach him to convert live Japanese fliers into dead ones.

Slim Jimmy Dowden, twenty-four, came from Colfax, Louisiana, was five feet eight inches tall and weighed about a hundred and fifty pounds. He had attended the University of California at Los Angeles for three and a half years before he quit to join the Navy. He was a typical Los Angeles youngster who turned out to be an excellent organizer and contrived to get a lot of work accomplished without even appearing to work. He proved surprisingly efficient as matériel officer, a job that requires energy and organizing ability. Jim Dowden had both, in spite of his singular fondness for lounging.

Flatley recalls: "I never did see him working. He was always stretched out, shooting the breeze with anyone who cared to argue, and apparently he never believed in wasting energy sitting up if he could lie down. But a checkup always showed that he had completed everything to be done in his department—and more besides. He seemed to have a system which got results, and after all, that's the thing that counts."

Of the four squadrons belonging to Air Group 10, the scouts, bombers and torpedo outfits had been equipped and begun organization several weeks before, but the fighters still lacked their Grumman Wildcats. Delivery was not expected for several days. Thoughtfully, Jim Flatley took this opportunity to grant leave to Vejtasa and Faulkner. He gave them each a week—all the time that could be spared, but not nearly enough for men who had gone through the kind of fighting they had endured. They understood, however, and were satisfied. Their week was spent looking for homes in Coronado to house their families. Vejtasa finally succeeded in getting a suitable place for his wife and their four-year-old son.

Flatley, who already had a home in Coronado, where he lived with his wife and young sons, did not take leave. There was too much work to be done.

At the end of ten days the eight young ensigns returned from sea duty and reported. With Swede's and Fritz's leaves up, there were now thirteen members of VF-10 on hand. Meanwhile the transfer requests of Pollock, Leppla and Edwards had been granted and they, too, would be ready for training in two and a half weeks. The squadron was beginning to take definite shape.

During the eighteen days of their voyage home, Flatley and the other airmen aboard had discussed at great length the question of American versus Japanese planes. They had delved into the relative merits of the Wildcat and the Zero. In Jim's mind there was no doubt that he had to base his combat tactics on fighting in formation, and on a plan most suitable to the performance of the Wildcat, in order to take fullest advantage of the Wildcat's better fire power, sound armor protection, self-sealing fuel tanks, faster diving speed and more rugged construction—against the greater speed, faster climb and maneuverability of the Zero.

Our fliers respected the Japanese fighter pilots' discipline, as well as their tactics (a tough formation in a fight) and ability to get the most from their planes' favorable performance. But they were equally aware of the weaknesses of Japanese planes, particularly their proneness to catch fire when hit by incendiaries.

Flatley and Lieutenant Commander James Thach, com-

Lieutenant Stanley "Swede" Vejtasa, who got three Jap planes in the Coral Sea battle, then went on to chalk up seven enemy planes shot down and one damaged in the Battle of Santa Cruz, believed to be a world record for a single fight. (*Wide World Photo*)

The carrier *Enterprise,* on which the Reapers were based much of the time, pointing its guns at Wake Island in the damaging raid of February 24th, 1942. (*Official U.S. Navy Photo*)

mander of VF-3 (to which Edward ("Butch") O'Hare belonged when he downed five Japs and damaged a sixth twin-engined bomber in February), had long been in agreement that there was no place in this war for the individualist. Our two great air tacticians had discovered early that "the lone wolf soon becomes the lost sheep," a creed similar to that adopted by Captain Eddie Rickenbacker in World War I.

For a great part of the return journey Flatley had been busy compiling the combat doctrine for his squadron, in which he incorporated his own experiences and those of other combat fighters who had fought against the Japanese. He devised special tactics to help his fighters meet all eventualities in the air. These he had set down on paper, accompanied by sketches of combat formations which were to be part of the indoctrination process for VF-10 squadron members.

There was yet the important question as to what name should be given the squadron other than the impersonal number which designated them. When Jim advanced "Grim Reapers" and asked me what I thought of it for a start, I had to agree that it was a good name. The insignia was to be a skeleton armed with a scythe. I took pencil and paper and made a rough outline of a skeleton, drew in a scythe held at full cock and gave the old boy a high-speed wing. Badly drawn as it was, the general effect stood the test. All that was missing now was a motto, and after deliberation we decided on "Mow 'em Down."

Jim had a more exact sketch made by Wilkes, an artist off the *Lex*, who was aboard our transport. In an hour he returned with an excellent drawing of the Grim Reaper, and in spite of Wilkes's denial, Flatley still insists that he can recognize himself in the drawing. A red circle was painted, then, around reaper and scythe, and the legend "Grim Reapers" was penciled in on top, with "Mow 'em Down" as a fitting counterpart at the bottom. Thus an insignia was born which came to be as feared as it was well known.

After our arrival, Wilkes painted a replica in a 45-degree power dive, with blood dripping from the scythe, on an eight-by-six-foot banner. This was fastened to the wall behind Flatley's desk, in full view of his squadron, whose goal was never to rest until all of the space on the banner was covered with small Jap flags, each designating confirmation of a hostile plane shot down by the squadron.

Other pictures—a tired and battered old Reaper sitting in a chair, with Reapers' Helpers (aircraftsmen) sweating over him, mending bullet holes, sharpening his scythe, tightening bolts, toiling on his air frame and armament—were slung up in the mechanics' and armorers' quarters.

It was a good insignia, all right, and meaningful.

Chapter 3

MIDWAY

WHILE FLATLEY organized his Reapers in San Diego, a powerful Japanese armada set out on an expedition intended to crown Nipponese conquests in the Far East. Instead, it ended in a rout and gave our forces one of the greatest naval victories in modern times.

Once the enemy withdrew from the Coral Sea it became evident that his intentions for a second drive lay in an entirely new direction. Where would the enemy advance to further his advantage? Where lay the biggest stumbling block? The answer to these questions was not really difficult.

The Hawaiian Islands protrude 3400 miles from our west coast into the Pacific and point directly at Japan. Pearl Harbor, our main naval operating base, is 2400 miles from the American mainland. Midway, some 1312 miles from Pearl Harbor, is only 2500 miles from Tokyo. As long as we held the Hawaiians, the enemy could scarcely hope to accomplish more than a raid on our west coast, even with naval superiority in the Pacific. However, if the Japanese seized even one of the bigger islands near Oahu, we would lose the use of Pearl Harbor as a base for fleet operations. Possession of the Hawaiians by Japan would not only seriously endanger the 7000-mile lifeline to Australia, the first 2400 miles of which depend on protection from Hawaii, but it would threaten our west coast.

The Japanese had the Hawaiians at their mercy by noon of December 7. Their well-laid scheme had come off, only we knew how well. Luckily, they did not follow through.

Their more immediate plans were far-reaching and focused on certain victory in the Far East. They judged their attack on Pearl Harbor as a mere first step for their invasion of Malaya, Burma, the Philippines and the Netherlands Indies; the slap at Hawaii was a preliminary one to assure the smooth working of more extensive operations to follow.

After their aircraft turned back, leaving our battleships sunk, burning or seriously impaired at their moorings, we began a systematic rebuilding of our Hawaiian defenses. The damaged ships were rushed into dock for repair, a long and tedious process. New battleships, already launched, were rushed to completion, but not until they were commissioned and released by the builders would we again have a battle line capable of trading blows with the powerful Japanese Navy. Our cruiser strength was good and we had six excellent aircraft carriers. The Japanese had a reported thirteen.

Our position was extremely delicate when Admiral Chester Nimitz relieved Rear Admiral Husband E. Kimmel, who had been in command of the Pacific Fleet at the outbreak of war. Nimitz was faced with the maintenance of long lines of communications, the defense of the strategically vital Hawaiians and Aleutians—all this with a temporary inferiority in naval power. Fortunately for us, we had found the right man for the job.

In a battleship-weak navy, aircraft carriers have to bear the brunt. Again we had the ideal commander: Vice Admiral (now Admiral) William Halsey. The Coral Sea battle had been the first encounter between aircraft carriers. Surface ships of the opposing fleets at no stage of the battle sighted each other. We successfully prevented the enemy from attaining his objective and proved the soundness of our concepts in the use of carriers, and of the air combat tactics developed by our naval air squadrons. True, the Japanese were no mean opponents, but our fliers were better, which helped to balance more closely the numerical difference in carrier strength.

The enemy knew we had seven carriers: the *Lexington,* *Yorktown, Wasp, Hornet, Ranger, Saratoga* and *Enterprise;* but the Japs calculated they would have to cope only with a few older battleship types, plus some cruisers and destroyers, for some time to come.

Before the war, our military defense of Hawaii had been concentrated on Oahu and on Midway. There were no appreciable number of troops stationed on the other main islands, nor were there any important airfields. Our defense, in accordance with pre-air power strategic concepts, consisted of a navy to prevent possible invasion and an army to defend the naval base should enemy landings be realized. The advent of aircraft never changed this outmoded theory drastically, except that we did add several hundred planes— fighters to defend against hostile bombers, and bombers to attack enemy ships at sea.

To the Japs the problem of invading the Hawaiian group must have appeared not overly difficult. The prize: absolute domination of the Pacific. The cost? If the venture succeeded, it would be well worth two hundred thousand men, and presumably, casualties would not run to anything near that number. Hawaii was the ripe plum that would fall into their laps.

The Jap command appeared to be certain that by the time we learned of their intentions the invading force would already be investing the islands, too late for our available carriers to interfere.

With all this evidence carefully weighed, the Japanese war lords gave the word to strike.

On June 2, carrier-borne Japanese reconnaissance planes flew over Dutch Harbor. In the afternoon a formation of Jap bombers followed and met unexpected American fighter opposition from a group of airmen, only recently

landed, who went up for the chase. The Japs escaped. It is
surmised that their carrier swung around through the Bering
Sea to give support to the invasion of the Aleutians at Kiska
and Attu.

We were on the alert. Secretary of War Henry L. Stimson
told Washington correspondents early in June that an attack
might be made on Alaska. On the west coast Lieutenant
General John L. De Witt had enforced a strict blackout during the latter part of May and had warned the population to
expect hostile attacks. There had been previous scares on the
west coast, some based on reality, like the shelling at Santa
Barbara by a Jap submarine in February, and others which
were merely the usual "snafu." The May-June preparations
somehow suggested something more.

If news of these alerts on the west coast and in Alaska
reached the Japanese—and there is every reason to believe
it did via our radio broadcasts—it shouldn't have worried
them at all, for according to their information, weren't we
without the means in the Pacific to stop them? Didn't we
lack the necessary carrier strength?

But consider, now, the situation on our own side. After
the fall of Wake, there had been a drive to increase the
number and quality of aircraft based on tiny Midway. The
Army at last had a handful of B-26s besides a few Flying
Fortresses for long-range, armed-patrol and high-level bombing. The Navy had moved in some dive bombers and torpedo planes to be manned by Navy, Marine and Army fliers.
In addition, the Navy kept a few Catalinas for long-range
patrol and to act as torpedo planes. The Marines had a small
number of Brewsters for fighter defense. More batteries of
coast defense guns and anti-aircraft weapons had been set
up and a small force of Marines and soldiers strengthened
the shore fortifications.

However, the small land area and the lack of cover and

space in which to disperse planes, gasoline, ammunition and other supplies somewhat reduced the effectiveness of the island as a base from which to wage an extended fight against an attacker equipped with twenty air squadrons and backed up by a powerful fleet of surface warships.

About June 2, several American aircraft carriers and their escorting warships steamed near Midway. They were prepared for battle and only awaited reports of the enemy's location before going into action.

On the morning of June 3 a lone Catalina cruised slowly through the skies seven hundred miles west of Midway. It had left the island long before dawn to reach the segment of Pacific it was assigned to search shortly after daylight. The lumbering Catalina was slightly south of due west of Midway when a member of its crew noticed smoke on the distant horizon. He rubbed his eyes and looked again. He made out, faintly, the superstructures of ships, whole long lines of them. The plane's radio cracked out a message. It was the first contact report. There was no need to identify the ships before reporting them "enemy," because we had no vessels in the area.

As the Catalina made a cautious approach, the big convoy grew slowly to vast proportions—five distinct columns, each stretching across almost five miles of ocean. The three center columns were made up of transports, ten of them, with two cruisers leading and two following astern. The two flanking columns were destroyers, some of them zigzagging through the sea ahead, sniffing for submarines.

In the radio shack on Midway, this startling news came "morsing" in piecemeal—first the contact with enemy ships, then the position, and then, as the crew of the Catalina got a closer look, the ships and their types. Not much time elapsed between these bits of information; the aerial scout must be curt and concise and, above all, speedy in transmitting his intelligence to base headquarters.

Midway's Senior Army Officer, Major General C. L. Tinker (who was lost when his plane failed to return on the last day of the action), chewed over the Catalina's information. A big enemy force was approaching, certainly, but where were the carriers and battleships? The enemy surely would not send out such a large fleet of thin-skinned vessels without air power and/or battleships to smash through the defenses.

At 10 A.M., nine Flying Fortresses were readied to intercept and deliver a light bombing attack. The crews climbed into their planes, revved up their engines, taxied in turn to the end of the runway, and to the silent wave-off of a grim-faced garrison, roared down the strip and set out for the target.

The flight was uneventful until they came in sight of the enemy. Then they circled, selected their targets, went hell-bent into the barrage of flak the ships threw up and made their bombing runs. Away went their sticks of bombs and soon the lead plane saw great geysers rise as the near misses exploded in the water among the ships. Two great balls of smoke and flame mushroomed up where bombs had scored hits. The first shots in the Battle of Midway had been fired.

With their job completed, the Fortress crews headed home, leaving a cruiser and a transport burning fiercely. Slighter damage had also been inflicted on other ships in the force.

The marine garrison was on its toes and flew security patrols of fighters against a possible lightning thrust by the enemy air striking force. The air crews waited, tense and expectantly, for the signal to climb into their dive bombers, torpedo planes and fighters.

All was quiet through the long afternoon, but no sooner had the men finished chow than four Catalinas started their engines, warmed up steadily and, with exhausts streaking blue flame, made their take-off run across the lagoon and rose into the night sky. Each flying boat carried a torpedo. Their assignment was to deliver a harrying night air-torpedo attack on the moonlit transports. The veteran crews navigated their planes uneventfully under the Pacific sky, checking on the octants from time to time by shooting the stars. Their long flight to the convoy, which had now steamed to within five hundred miles of Midway, was routine and without incident.

Eventually the Catalinas reached their target. Trained eyes picked up the long wakes of the ships, and throttling down the engines, they glided in to attack. The big planes, soundless except for the noise of air passing over their metal skins, swept across the destroyers in the flanking column; it was the transports they were after. The blacked-out ships opened fire on the shadows flashing past. Nevertheless, the planes dropped their "fish," scoring hits on one or two large vessels, one of which was believed sunk.

Long before daybreak on June 4, both sides were swinging into action.

As dawn neared and the escorting Nipponese warships knifed through the long swells, Jap airmen climbed into their planes and coursed down the flight decks. The first light of the morning sun glinted on the big red discs painted on the wings of their aircraft as they sped for Midway. They came in above twenty thousand feet. As they neared their objective, they dropped their noses and slanted down, making a full-power glide approach. The Japs thought they were getting away with it.

Back on Midway, even before the enemy pilots had prepared to take off, American naval patrol planes were launched before dawn and fanned out spokewise. Each pilot had his own particular sector. The fliers were looking for more Jap columns; on the previous night they had noticed only the big convoy. Knowing that the enemy must be bringing in carriers to blast a landing for the troops, they sought them now.

As the first rays of light leaped skyward, one of the scouts found what they had all been seeking. There on the horizon rose the pagodalike structures of Japanese battleships and the characteristic shape of long, high-decked flat-tops. The radioman tapped out the ships' position, course, speed and number. No sooner was the report out than Zeros were on the scout's tail. A running fight ensued. Enemy fighters, defending the main fleet, tried too late to nail the scout; his message was already through. The Zeros attacked with waspish persistency but never succeeded in getting past the scout's rear gunner, nor at the pilot, who fought with his front guns.

Midway exploded into a scene of intense activity as the report came in. Twenty-seven dive bombers, sixteen Fortresses, ten torpedo planes and about forty fighters queued up to get on the take-off strip. One after the other the machines roared down the runway, rose into the air and headed for the enemy in small groups. When the first hostile formations appeared a short time later, all except the Marine fighter squadrons assigned to defend Midway had flown off the island. The Japanese hope of destroying our attack planes on the ground had been thwarted.

Marine combat patrol fighters recorded first sight contact with the incoming Jap planes twenty miles from Midway. As the Marines tried to dive their Brewsters through to get at the bombers, screening Zeros fought them off. For the next thirty minutes the biggest air battle fought by American and Japanese fliers up to that time raged over and around Midway. The defenders shot down more than forty enemy machines and suffered such heavy losses of their own that only a few returned to Midway.

The more than two hundred attacking planes finally penetrated our much smaller number and continued to come in closer. Midway's anti-aircraft batteries let fly. Still the Japs came on. Their bombers dived into range of the lighter guns, the automatics. At that point our Marine and Army gunners began to exact a heavy toll. But the Japanese pressed their attack home with great determination. They bombed everything in sight, carefully "missing" the strip of fine runway, no doubt on orders to keep it intact for the use of their own planes after the island was captured.

The sky was a mass of aircraft. Burning machines fell on the island and into the sea for miles around. Into this thirty-minute blitz the enemy had thrown a greater force than that used against Pearl Harbor. He demolished buildings, set fire to supplies and killed some of our fighting men, but he sank no ships and destroyed no planes on the ground, as he had at Oahu.

Our Marine fighter pilots made the enemy earn every American aircraft downed. Estimated Japanese losses were two machines for each American fighter shot out of the sky.

Scarcely had the Jap attack groups sighted Midway when our attack squadrons sighted the Jap fleet. They attacked at once. Swarms of Zeros tried to intercept, but in spite of the Japs' furious efforts, our planes continued to press within range of the ships' guns and then through the violent barrage thrown up by the whole fleet.

Six Navy TBF torpedo planes sought out two enemy carriers and scored a hit. Only one of these planes survived.

Sixteen Marine dive bombers attacked a carrier and scored three hits. Eight of them were lost.

Another group of eleven Marine dive bombers attacked a battleship, scoring two hits. Fires started and caused the ships to list.

A sixteen-plane section of Fortresses made a high-level bombing attack on the carriers and scored three hits. One flat-top was noted smoking heavily.

The first phase of the Battle of Midway was over; the enemy had taken a beating, but it wasn't heavy enough. Although the Japs had failed to effect a surprise and had not succeeded in annihilating Midway's air squadrons on the ground, they had endured the island's counter-punches with surprisingly light injury. They kept on closing in after the last of our attacking planes retired.

The enemy's heavy anti-aircraft barrage and the throngs of defending Zeros had much reduced our own fire power and had cost us many aircraft. But the remaining planes of Midway's squadrons were able to land, refuel and rearm—thanks to the Japs' solicitude in preserving the runway. Then they went back to the attack.

The Jap fleet, when last spotted by our air striking force, had been approximately two hundred miles northwest of and standing in toward Midway. At that time the American carriers were roughly the same distance from the island as the Japanese. The enemy was still too far away to be reached by our carriers' aircraft.

As soon as the main Japanese fleet had been located, the American commander ordered his whole force on a course that would bring him in between the Japanese and their target. Our ships, by maintaining this new course, would come in eventually directly between the Jap striking and occupation forces. As they steamed along converging lines, every mile advanced closed the range. By closing in and attacking the enemy carriers, and by putting them out of action, our carrier force could then menace the convoy of transports. Once these soft targets without air cover were brought into range, they would be easy meat for our pilots.

For a couple of hours we lost sight of the Japanese fleet. But if the enemy's course and speed had been calculated correctly, and if the course plotted by our force was exact, we would be in position to deliver our air blow by 9 A.M. At that time squadrons of dive bombers, torpedo planes and escort

fighters were launched. The Navy was entering the scrap.
Fidgety fighter patrols hovered overhead while the ships
pushed in toward the enemy, awaiting the reports of their
squadrons.

Nearly two hours passed before the first sign appeared
that all was not well. Squadrons which had reached the area
where the Japs were expected to be found no trace of the
enemy. Slowly and methodically they cruised and searched.
For an hour they burned precious fuel, every minute of it
lessening their chances to fly back to the carriers.

Lieutenant Commander C. W. McCluskey, *Enterprise*
air group commander, had arrived where the enemy should
have been and, unable to locate the Jap warships, continued
his search. Weaving back and forth, closely scrutinizing
the horizon, he followed this search pattern for about an
hour. Then in the distance, to starboard, he saw smoke. The
enemy lay before him and his squadrons. Even as his
radioman broadcast the foe's position, it became clear what
the Japs had been up to. Having failed to surprise and raze
Midway's air attack group, bruised by bombs and torpedoes
and the unexpected heavy loss of bombers and fighters in
the first assault, they had made an about turn instead of continuing to Midway. Now they were hastening for the cover
of the northern overcast.

Presumably the Japs hoped to hide out for the remainder
of the day and then once more curve south, this time
to eradicate Midway's planes in a night air attack. There is
also the likelihood that enemy submarines had reported the
position of our carriers, and that the Japs were trying to re-
enter the fog bank so that they could engage our carrier
force from a position of comparative security.

It is one of those fascinating historical "ifs" to speculate
what might have happened if Commander McClusky had
turned his group back toward our ships, or headed for Midway as the *Hornet* group had done, instead of persisting until

he found the Jap fleet. Almost certainly there would have been no Battle of Midway, and possibly all of our carriers would have gone to the bottom with the *Yorktown*. After he found the enemy, no contact reports flashed back; there was dead radio silence until Commander McClusky gave the attack order to his group.

At almost the same time Torpedo 8 from the *Hornet* led by Lieutenant Commander John Waldron, located the enemy; all squadrons launched simultaneously from other carriers were nearly out of gas. Most were too far from their flat-tops to make the return flight. Some units stretched their diminishing gas supply and tried to land on Midway to refuel and re-enter the battle from that point. Several sorely needed planes and airmen were lost to us in forced landings, although some of the survivors were picked up later.

Torpedo Squadron 8 deployed and made its approach at water level. The planes were alone, at the mercy of every Zero, and the target of every gun on the Jap warships. There were no fighters to engage the Zeros and split up the anti-aircraft fire.

Torpedo 8 headed in through a terrific barrage of exploding missiles, and so low that the battleships were able to fire their 14-inch, 1460-pound shells into the water ahead of them. Hundreds of tons of ocean sprang into the air, reaching up like giant hands and hurling the oncoming planes into the sea. All were downed before they reached the torpedo release point—except for one.

This single torpedo plane, flown by Ensign G. H. Gay, found itself completely alone. There in front, in a smoky haze, lay the enemy ships. Gay selected a carrier, aimed his plane and loosed the torpedo. Even as it sped under water toward its target, Gay's machine staggered through the air. It had been hit but kept going well enough to slosh into the sea gently, enabling Gay to get out before its ripped and tangled framework sank. Bobbing up and down amid enemy warships, Gay grabbed a floating seat cushion and hit his head underneath. He feared, and rightly, that the Japanese might make short work of him if they thought he was alive. By this action he helped save his life.

Torpedo 8 went to its doom in the finest American Navy tradition. It sighted the enemy. It attacked. It went to its death trying. No more could be expected of any fighting unit.

Fatal as the valiant final gesture of Torpedo 8 had been, the squadron carried out to the letter the creed which Skipper Waldron had instilled in his men. From the first he had been adamant that if the going got tough and the squadron was being attacked, the others—plane by plane and right through to the last machine—must strive to continue whatever task the squadron had been sent out to accomplish. His men carried John Waldron's creed into the red seas of Midway—to the last man and the last plane.

In the meantime dive bombers from the *Yorktown* and *Enterprise* had picked their targets and were maneuvering into diving position.

Fighter Squadron 3, led by one of our foremost flyers, Lieutenant Commander Jimmy Thach, escorted the *Yorktown's* torpedo planes. Arriving simultaneously with the *Yorktown's* dive bombers, both squadrons spread and fell upon the enemy in proper form, attacking from above and all around the circle. Fighting 3 prevented the Zeros from picking off our bombardment aircraft. Jap gunners, instead of being able to concentrate on a single formation, were faced with planes coming in from above and all sides, forcing them to divert the fire of their guns into several directions. As soon as the torpedo planes began their run the air appeared to be filled with Zeros. Some high up were battling our dive bombers, others came low after the torpedo planes.

Thach, having split his six fighters into three two-plane

sections, was about two thousand feet above the TBDs when
down came the first formation of Zeros—twenty-four of them.
According to Jimmy, the Zeros came from above and astern
all at once. One after the other they sloped down, each
shooting at a Wildcat in his approach, then flattening out
and hauling up in a climb as he passed, easing into position
for another high pass.

The six Americans stayed with the Zeros to keep them
from making a high-side assault on the torpedo planes, while
the TBD gunners handled those trying for a horizontal attack. Meanwhile, the torpedo planes came in further. Soon
they would be near enough to drop their "fish."

Just then Thach saw another group of fourteen Zeros
headed for the torpedo planes, trying for a high frontal
attack from a starboard sweep. The swirling formations of
Yank and Jap fighters had battled right into and through the
heavy AA barrage and the network of tracers from the Jap
ships. Presently Jimmy called his fighters off the first group
of Zeros and had them spread out to meet the fourteen newcomers. Again the American fighters interposed themselves
between the second force of Zeros and our TBDs. Again all
the fury of the Jap fighters was thrown against the sturdy
Wildcats, but the American fighters were at their peak. The
Japs were beaten back.

Our torpedo planes swept within range. They broke up
into three groups, each selecting a different target. One after
the other, the TBDs plumped their 21-inch (diameter) torpedoes, and cleaving through the sea, the missiles hit their
mark. Great waterspouts rose from the sides of three carriers.

Our planes re-formed on the far side of the fleet. They
had fought their way through and delivered their torpedoes,
smashing gaping holes in the hulls of the carriers. It was a
striking performance. The squadron had accomplished its
mission successfully.

While the torpedoes crashed into the Japanese flat-tops,

Enroute toward Tokyo in April, 1942, the *Enterprise* moves along beside the *Hornet*, her scout bombers lined up on the flight deck for instant take-off. The object of this mission was to place Doolittle's bombers within range of Tokyo. (*Official U. S. Navy Photo*)

Action in the Battle of Midway. Note smoke from shot-down enemy plane at right, and boats in water fast moving cruiser (left) and destroyer (right).

heavy bombs delivered by our dive bombers tore into them from above. The *Akagi, Kaga* and *Soryu* were ablaze. Many of their planes, caught on the decks, were afire. Two battleships had been hit; one was burning fiercely. A destroyer had been struck by a bomb which is believed to have sunk it.

Ensign Gay, still adrift, had a ringside view. He watched the carriers break into flame and observed several stricken warships slow down. He beheld our attack groups battering away at the enemy vessels and saw Jap aircraft crash into the water all around him. The fourth enemy carrier, the *Hiryu,* was still at large. She had an attack group of thirty-six planes in the air. About 1:30 A.M., eighteen of her dive bombers spotted and attacked the *Yorktown* task force. The few air-borne Wildcats of Fighting 3, aided by some *Hornet* fighters, intercepted. The Jap bombers lasted long enough to pierce the fighter defense. Down slipped their bombs . . . one . . . two . . . three of them, all scoring hits on the *Yorktown.* They detonated below her flight deck. Three times the great vessel erupted; then she stopped dead. A column of smoke enveloped her. Moments ago she had been swinging hard to either beam as she evaded the bombs; now she lay stock still.

But she recovered quickly. A wave of relief surged through the tense watchers on other ships as the *Yorktown* began to move forward again. She turned back on her course and operations were resumed. Her fighters were circling to come aboard for fuel and ammunition when a second wave of Jap aircraft attacked. This time they were torpedo planes —Aichis, twelve of them. They came in low, hugging the surface of the sea in their approach. Our air-borne fighters winged out to intercept. The guns of every warship within range opened up. Seven of the Jap planes dropped into the sea, but five came through to release their torpedoes. They were shot down almost at once, but not soon enough.

The *Yorktown* had not been moving rapidly. She had been using only part of her power and could not dodge as easily as she had so many times before. One of the torpedoes smashed into her hull, blasting an enormous hole. She began to take on a violent list. Her returning planes were warned to proceed to point so-and-so, land on carrier such-and-such. Some of the fliers did not have enough fuel, so they rolled up their wheels and splashed into the sea near friendly destroyers.

Although she had a dangerous list, the *Yorktown* was not yet sinking. Captain Buckmaster ordered his crew to abandon ship. They went overside and were picked up by escorting warships. At least 90 per cent of her crew was transferred safely and many of her planes found a resting place on the *Hornet*. All night they stayed around, guarding the tilted hull of their beloved flat-top.

Midway's morning air losses had been restored to some extent by the arrival of carrier planes which were too low on fuel to return to their ships. Late in the afternoon the planes took off again to lash out against the crippled Jap fleet. Before sunset they came upon and struck at some of the smoking vessels. Three bomb hits were scored on a flat-top (probably the *Akagi*), which was already burning. Another strike was made on a second large ship and a further bomb struck a large cruiser, rekindling her fires. One destroyer got into the line of fire and took a heavy bomb which is believed to have sunk her.

The carrier *Hiryu* was located shortly before this wave from Midway swept over the enemy warships, and the carrier air striking force was sent out at 4:30 P.M. to eliminate this last floating base.

Scouting 8, a companion force to the lost Torpedo Squadron 8, skippered by Lieutenant Commander William J. ("Gus") Widhelm, took off from the *Hornet* to join in the attack. Widhelm's force followed closely astern of the *Enterprise* planes, which arrived first over the target. By the time the *Hornet's* VSB-8 reached its 20,000-foot attack perch, the Japs' AA was exploding all around the big *"E's"* bombers. Still their bombs kept on scoring. Then Widhelm's bombers went in to complete the job. Of his thirteen planes, seven scored hits.

By 6 P.M. the *Hiryu* was a badly battered wreck. Engulfed by flames, she was unable to proceed further. The enemy fleet, indeed, no longer existed. A Jap cruiser had dealt the death blow to one of the sinking carriers and an American sub eased herself inside the Jap formation during the evening and finished off the foundering *Soryu*. Before morning, three flat-tops of the Jap striking force were no more.

The *Hiryu*, a burning hulk, drifted helplessly through the night. Two damaged battleships, one little better than a derelict, sought slowly to escape. At least one destroyer had been sunk and one transport was believed sunk by a torpedo from one of our Catalinas.

In the twelve daylight hours of June 4 the American force had administered the greatest defeat ever suffered by the Japanese Imperial Navy. Yamamoto's hopes of invading and occupying the Hawaiian Islands had, with his ships, gone to the bottom of the Pacific. His surviving warships were escaping as fast as they could to the safety of the northern fog bank.

As June 5 dawned, planes from American carriers and from Midway ranged the skies, seeking out remnants of the defeated Jap fleet. They hit first upon the *Hiryu*. She came into sight near where she had been attacked the evening before and was sent to a wet grave quickly and with dispatch. She was the Jap striking force's fourth and last carrier.

The powerful naval force which had broken through the fog only twenty-four hours before now dragged its pommeled ships back across the Pacific in headlong flight. During the night it had broken up into small groups, one or two destroyers escorting a limping battleship or cruiser. Some of the vessels had lost all contact with each other. Each was making its best speed, abandoning the rest to their fate.

Bereft of carriers, the retreating fleet was easy prey. There were no enemy planes nor airmen to offer opposition. Those that had not been shot out of the air had died on the ocean, like exhausted land birds, after their gasoline gave out. Some had gone down with their carriers. Without air opposition, the task of killing off the disorganized Japs was not too difficult, once they were found.

Meanwhile, our carriers steamed westward, hunting for the occupation force which was scurrying homeward, while our air squadrons scanned the ocean to the north for stragglers of the enemy striking fleet. The *Hornet* was busily engaged in this chase. With her air department considerably strengthened by the newly acquired *Yorktown* fliers, she was ready for a killing but unfortunately could find only one light cruiser, which she promptly sank.

The *Enterprise* had better luck. Her air squadrons were actively engaged on some Jap ships and helped dispatch a heavy cruiser.

During the night the airmen had a respite from their long hours of hard flying, but they were at it again early on June 6. The boys dropped two 1000-pound and one 500-pound bomb squarely on a Jap battle wagon, and spilled two more 1000-pounders within fifty feet, inflicting additional damage. A heavy cruiser caught two 1000-pounders and a similar missile fell on the fantail of a destroyer. By way of a fillip to this action, four Wildcats teamed up to strafe a destroyer. Their sixteen .50-caliber machine guns sprayed the Japs at their guns and at fire control stations.

After a brief pause to refuel and rearm, the planes struck at two other Jap cruisers and a pair of destroyers scattered more than a hundred miles apart. A half dozen 1000-

pounders descended on one cruiser, another hit its companion, and a third projectile struck a destroyer. The first cruiser was completely gutted by fire and its crew was abandoning ship when our planes left the scene. No more need be said about a destroyer which has been on the receiving end of a 1000-pound bomb.

Midway was awakened on June 5 by a few light shells. A Jap submarine had edged close to the shore and loosed a few rounds of fire. Our shore batteries, whose gunners had waited impatiently for a target, took the opportunity to reply. This small exchange of gunfire was the sole occasion during the entire battle in which American and Japanese guns were near enough to each other for a shooting match.

During the morning some of our Fortresses off Midway located several damaged battleships and cruisers west of the island. They scored two bomb hits on a cruiser. One of the bombs apparently locked the cruiser's steering gear, and the stricken ship began to spin in tight circles. It was so badly smashed and listing that it probably sank. A second wave of Midway's Army bombers blasted a second cruiser in this group.

Again and again small formations, stringing out from Midway, were rewarded for their untiring search. Marines reported a hit on a cruiser which had been crippled by the Army just before noon. During midafternoon, in worsening weather, three Fortresses scored three bomb hits on still another cruiser.

Gus Widhelm's scout bombers roared out that day from the *Hornet*, searching for the *Hiryu* they had hit at 6 P.M. the day before, and for a battleship which had been left ablaze. They picked up two broad, thick oil wakes and followed their quarry like bloodhounds. At the end of a fifty-mile trail of slick there were two great patches of oil and Jap sailors were floating in the sea. Some other squadron had beaten them to the job. When Gus was asked afterward

whether he made an attempt to pick off any of the Jap sailors, he remarked quietly that there were no bullets to waste.
Gus's men searched the area further and discovered a destroyer leaving the graveyard. They were preparing to attack
again when a second group of bombers got in ahead once
more. Twice frustrated, Gus and his men had to find themselves something else to bomb.

The *Enterprise* and *Hornet* had continued west through
the night in pursuit of Jap warships. On the sixth our carrier
squadrons again attacked enemy vessels, two of which were
identified as the heavy cruisers *Mikuma* and *Mogami*.

Of these assaults, Gus Widhelm says: "We scouted on the
morning of the sixth from the *Hornet* and found the cruisers
Mogami and *Mikuma* and four destroyers. We made two
separate attacks, leaving the *Mogami* sinking after the first,
and returning later to finish the *Mikuma*. While we were at
it we added two destroyers to the total.

"One of them we collected through the error of Ensign
Horner. Pushing over to dive at the *Mikuma*, the kid pushed
the button which let down his wheels, instead of the control that would set his diving flaps. Because his wheels did
not offer as much drag as the flaps, Horner was diving faster
than the rest of us. He realized at once the danger of being
shot at by one of his own boys, because we have a rule to
protect ourselves from Zeros that might dive on us during
an attack, and that rule says we must shoot at any plane
going down faster than our own machines.

"The kid hauled out of this dive, rolled up his wheels, and
then turned right back into his dive, this time lowering his
flaps. The few seconds he was flattened out, making the
correction, carried him across the cruiser, and when he
pointed down again, he found himself directly over one
of the destroyers. So he lined the vessel up in his sights and
landed his bomb there. When it hit, the Jap destroyer
jumped up in the air, turned over and sank—just like that.

It didn't even stay long enough to have its picture taken for the Navy archives."

Gus laid his own 1000-pounder right alongside the *Mogami's* funnel. His fellow fliers, who watched from above, still argue as to which side was struck by the bomb.

Gus then flew back to the *Hornet* to rearm. As soon as he returned to the Jap cruisers he plumped a bomb toward the *Mogami's* bow, about on the forward turret. By this time two destroyers, one at her bow and one at her stern, were taking survivors off the *Mogami*, with the *Mikuma* standing by. Before polishing off the *Mikuma* our pilots had a good look at the show while they were selecting the best wind angle. They finally turned over and dived down wind, scoring eleven hits on the *Mikuma*, which sent her to the bottom. Then, in shallow dives, they gave the destroyers a good working over with their fixed wing guns and the free twin .30-calibers manned by the rear gun-radio operators.

Gus says: "We were down so low that we could see the decks of the ships crowded with Japs; hundreds of rescued survivors were packed in tight all over the place. They ran around trying to escape our machine-gun bullets, which ripped along their decks. Before starting out on this flight our fixed guns had been loaded with armor-piercing bullets. Tracers and incendiaries had been left out purposely.

"Suddenly a shell exploded so close to me that the blast rolled my plane half over. A fragment of shell evidently cut my oil lines because everything turned black, oil poured into the cockpit and my engine quit working properly. I turned away and warned my radio operator, George D. Stokely, to prepare for a water landing. He yelled, 'Okay,' and continued firing at a destroyer with his free guns. I repeated: 'Get ready for a water landing.' He called back, 'Are you hurt?' I shouted that I wasn't. He answered again, 'Okay,' and reopened fire on the Japs.

"Although I was afraid we would crash, my engine recovered some of its power and brought us slowly back to our ship at last. I sent the carrier a forced-landing signal because I had to get aboard on the first approach. There wasn't enough power coming from the engine to take me away for a second approach if the carrier gave me a wave-off. The carrier didn't seem overanxious for me to try the landing— my flaps and wheels wouldn't work—but I landed anyway. Inspecting the plane later, I discovered that all the intake stacks had been knocked loose by the blast of that shell. It sure was a close one.

"Stokely, I think, got a lot of Japs in our sweeps. He's a wild man with a gun. Once, at Noumea, he hit a running deer right behind the ear with a rifle bullet. That's shooting!"

The *Yorktown* was still afloat on the morning of the sixth. Captain Buckmaster arranged for some volunteers to get back aboard and ready her to be towed into Pearl Harbor. This was probably the first time since the days of wooden vessels that a warship, damaged in action, was abandoned, only to have her captain return aboard and attempt to salvage her twelve hours later.

In the afternoon the destroyer *Hamman* pulled alongside the *Yorktown* and began transferring men and salvage gear to the carrier. Unobserved, a Jap sub drew near and shot out three torpedoes. They all struck home. Two made contact with the *Yorktown* dead ahead and astern of the *Hamman*, while the third hit the *Hamman* straight amidships as she lay alongside. It smashed into her hull and lifted her decks, killing many of her crew. The powerful blasts of the torpedo hits on the *Yorktown* added to the casualties of the small warship, which sank at once. This fresh damage ended all further attempts to save the big carrier. She settled more rapidly this time, and early on June 7 she went under.

The Battle of Midway was ended. A careful count showed that our fliers had sunk four aircraft carriers, two heavy 8500-

ton cruisers, three destroyers and one or more transports. An estimated 275 enemy aircraft were destroyed, and an extremely conservative estimate showed that 4800 Japs were killed or drowned.

On the damaged list were three battleships (one so severely that she was believed sunk); three heavy cruisers, at least one severely; one light cruiser, three destroyers and three transports or auxiliary vessels.

Our losses were one destroyer, one aircraft carrier and a death list of 92 officers and 215 enlisted men.

Chapter 4

INDOCTRINATION

THE FIRST real combat between American and Japanese air forces approximately equal in modernity and strength was fought in the Battle of the Coral Sea. While the Japanese were advancing through Malaya, Burma, the Philippines and the Netherlands Indies, there had never been adequate planes available to meet the enemy on equal terms. Japanese air squadrons, in overwhelming numbers, proceeded to blast a path for closely following landing troops. Allied air opposition was unprepared and had no chance against these drives. Consequently there grew up the myth of the Zero, which persisted until Japanese and American air forces clashed on equal terms.

The lessons our air groups learned in early May 1942 were the basis from which our counter-tactics developed. Midway, one month later, added to this knowledge because the action disclosed rather clearly how the Japanese stacked up in the air.

Pilots who fought against the Zeros were impressed by the Jap plane's steep, fast climb, its flexibility and speed, but they also noted its incinerator-like quality; it flared up like a matchbox whenever it was hit.

Jim Flatley had no illusions about the matter. The Wildcat was the only plane he had to fight with, and it was his job to devise tactics which would enable his fighter to overcome the Zero. As he put it, "I was not prepared to sacrifice armor, self-sealing tanks and the excellent fire power of a hard-hitting battery of .50-caliber guns embedded in the wings of the Wildcat for an unarmored plane that breaks into flame as soon as its gasoline tanks have been hit.

"In the Wildcat," he added, "we had a solid and dependable machine whose armor protected us against bullets fired from directly astern and whose engine could not be shot up either by the Zero's explosive 20-mm. shells or the small 7.7-caliber bullets. Our pilots came home unhurt although their planes were sieved with bullet holes. We had efficient self-sealing fuel tanks, and what's more, they functioned. Not a single one of our Wildcats ever caught fire.

"At low altitudes we could almost keep up with the Zero and our heavier wing loading enabled us to dive faster. The Wildcat's rugged construction allowed it to dive on full throttle—something the Zero could not do because the strain would rip off its wing."

Combat pilots generally concede that, if necessary, it is not only wise but advisable to sacrifice some performance if the sacrifice will let them outstay the enemy in the air, i.e., will let them carry more fuel and ammunition, which weighs the plane down and therefore makes it less maneuverable. A fighter plane, after it has used up its ammunition, has no more bite than a baby without teeth.

As for the human element, Jim Flatley declared: "Our fliers shot with considerably more accuracy than the average Japanese. This was of prime importance, because it meant that when we did secure a proper position to attack we shot the enemy down every time. And our planes did not break up in mid-air. We knew it would take a while before we could expect all of us to be supplied with the fine new fighters that were being built. Meanwhile, we had to get on with the war. The smart thing was to evolve air combat tactics that would make the Jap fight the way we wanted him to."

Flatley proceeded to do "the smart thing." Combat reports collected from scores of pilots gave him a well-rounded, complete and accurate picture of the enemy's methods. Tirelessly he tested and retested new theories translated into new flying formations. Before long he was satisfied that he had the answer to the Zero.

Naturally, Jim took considerable interest in each man assigned to VF-10. His job was to build a strong team of fighters, something like building up a football team except that a weak fighter, unlike a weak player, has no bench on which to sit out the game. A weak link in the chain, he is prone to expose himself too easily by rashness or ineptitude. Several weak members may lose the squadron more men than it can afford, and thus lose the battle.

The service, therefore, sorts its applicants carefully. If they pass the rigid physical tests and entrance examinations, the young Navy students are sent to pre-flight schools. After a tough training course they go on to flight school. Eventually a percentage of these men, perhaps a little more than half, qualify and get their wings. Then they are assigned to centers where they get practice in advanced flying, meteorology, combat tactics, gunnery, navigation, engineering and the other subjects an efficient airman needs to know. In prewar years a flier then served duty with various squadrons, which gradually gave him experience in every type of plane. Today, when it is necessary to compress the training period, the air force makes rough selections as to what types of aircraft the fledgling fliers are best adapted to, and most needed for, and fits them accordingly into the several branches. This enables the up-and-coming combat pilot to give his whole attention to the specific job for which he is best suited, be it in fighters, bombers, torpedo or scout planes, or in big flying boats.

This is a most important advance, one equally as significant as the notable step taken in 1932, when our Navy, alone of the world navies, opened flying schools to senior officers. Many of our present admirals—such men as Ernest

King, William Halsey and Frederick Sherman—learned to fly at that time, with thousands of other sea officers who won their wings to be better prepared for the command and operation of ships in a modern sea-air era.

X Men who entered the Navy via the naval flying reserve were able to skip the full naval course in order to concentrate the main part of their studies on flying subjects. This was the case with many of the young men assigned to VF-10. In training them, Commander Flatley started on the premise that if he were going to be successful he would first have to build up plenty of confidence—confidence in themselves and confidence in their equipment and tactics. He reasoned that, if they had that much, good morale would follow.

One of his major objectives was to develop leadership in the boys from the outset. As a carrier fighter, the pilot never knows when he will have to take over a flight, when he must assume the lead in battle. For that reason Flatley impressed upon his young Reapers the moral responsibility vested in them, and he taught them all there was to be taught about flying, as well as the handling of enlisted personnel. He asked them to assume that they were to be the squadron commanders of tomorrow.

This, too, was an important point. In the peacetime Navy many years would elapse before a man could rise to command and the youngsters taken in as reserves could scarcely hope to be more than fliers. To help them over this mental hurdle, Flatley made the boys take turns leading training flights and sent them out on their own. As soon as they understood tactics he made them plan flights and take charge.

Jim's five fundamental requirements for a successful squadron were set forth this way: leadership, morale, sound training and plenty of it, piloting efficiency, matériel efficiency. "They are all closely bound together. For the lack of one, the rest will fall through. Stress each and they all add up to the whole."

He made it clear that his idea of a good leader was not a man who was a good leader only in the air, but one who possessed other necessary characteristics, such as patience, kindness and loyalty. A good leader, he said, must have ability and a thorough knowledge of the professional aspects of his job. The squadron leader must be the best, or at least as good as, the best pilot in the squadron. He must retain complete control at all times in all squadron activities. He must lead all the way and maintain initiative. He must give each man a chance to develop. He must treat each man as an individual and must stress a cheerful attitude.

Jim did not neglect to point out to his men that they were going to fight a lengthy war and couldn't count on being back in six months or even a year. "We are going out to fight as long as we are needed," he told them. To eliminate any doubt about the matter, he told wives and sweethearts bluntly not to look for any of them for at least two years.

Morale—"the ability to withstand the most rigorous conditions and to come up with a smile," as Flatley defined it— was exceedingly good among his boys. Jim was particularly insistent on a smart squadron, for "a good smart outfit gets along without accidents." The Reapers made a nearly perfect score in this respect; in the entire four months' training period, they had only four minor accidents in landings and take-offs, and in carrier operations from October to February they recorded only one accident on deck and one forced landing in the water.

Flatley achieved that degree of efficiency by harping continually on the value of knowing planes, particularly the power plant, on keeping a cool head regardless of emergency, on the danger of becoming overconfident, and by watching personally for overconfidence. He appealed to individual pride to keep the planes flying, because a machine cracked up even temporarily means damage and loss of use of equipment, which in time of war is an unpardonable sin.

"Squadron commanders," Jim said, "must try to anticipate accidents if it is possible, and must at very frequent intervals go over landing and take-off technique, use of oxygen, radio aids, power-plant operations and such matters."

When there were no accidents over too long a period, instead of congratulating himself and his squadron, Jim took extra precaution to prevent smugness and possible laxness, for "a plane is treacherous; it throws you as soon as you lose respect for it." One thing Jim demanded: there was to be no "flat-hatting"; they could do all the fancy flying they liked at altitude, but it was an unforgivable offense to be caught showing off when flying low. He didn't want the rugged individualist nor the sourpuss; he discussed this at the beginning and claims he never had any.

On the qualifications of a fighter pilot, such highly qualified combat pilots as Commanders Flatley and Thach are in agreement. The prospective fighter pilot must have first, and above everything else, the desire to become a fighter pilot. He must devote all his attention to keeping fit, and develop his flying and shooting until he is a true professional. There is no future for an amateur; he doesn't live long enough.

A fighter pilot must have or develop a keen instinct to kill. His job is to shoot down hostile planes and to take every possible advantage of his foe's shortcomings. He must develop this instinct to a fine point, must become a hunter who stalks his prey in the air, who is out to destroy. Under no circumstances must an enemy, caught at a disadvantage, be allowed to escape. The maxims on this matter run: "The enemy who gets away today may be the one who will shoot you down tomorrow—or one of your comrades. There is no chivalry in this war and there is no place for it." It is important to the squadron that every menacing plane is shot out of the sky without delay, if possible, and therefore it is vital that the fighter pilot practice gunnery until he can hit his flying target with one short burst. One day his life may depend on that one burst.

Both Flatley and Thach emphasize that in shooting exercises it is not sufficient for the fighter pilot to get some strikes on the target sleeve. He must put most of his bullets into it, and even then, anything less than 100 per cent is subject to improvement. The pilot should practice until he can put all his bullets where he wants them, regardless of his angle of approach.

Most fighter pilots with three or four planes to their credit would down many times that number if they were top-notch marksmen. Men like Major Joe Foss, the Marine ace, have high scores because they seldom miss.

A smooth flying performance is considered another prerequisite for the combat pilot. He must train until he flies almost subconciously. There is no such thing as a born flier. It is said that sound knowledge of the plane and extensive practice and concentration will enable a man who has the necessary co-ordination merely to "wish" his plane into a certain position and it appears to get there. When an airman reaches that state, he merits the common term "a natural flier"—one to whom the engine, wings and controls of his plane have become almost as much a part of him as his fingers and toes.

The fighter pilot must be alert mentally. Every member of the squadron has to have the sharp perception of a potential quarterback. In the fast changing formations and ever altering balances of air combat, he must recognize instantly when to go on the defensive, as well as when to change to the offensive. Failure to lance in and take out an opponent might mean the death of a comrade, or several comrades. His ability to know when to attack should result in the field's being cleared, speedily, of opponents. On his judg--

A Japanese heavy cruiser of the Mogami class, after it was bombed by American carrier-based naval aircraft in the Battle of Midway. (*Official U.S. Navy Photo*)

Interior of one of the hangars on Midway Island, damaged during the battle of June 4th, 5th and 6th, 1942. (*Official U. S. Navy Photo*)

ment and on his ability to take advantage of every opening may rest the outcome of battle.

These and many other highly essential traits make it nearly impossible for the flying instructor alone to determine whether a new student will make the grade. The instructor's job is to teach him to fly a plane. Others take him step by step onward. Only when the candidate joins a squadron, where he will be taken up by the commander and other battle-experienced pilots, will it be evident whether he is fighter-pilot material.

With these things in mind, it is easy to understand how carefully Flatley watched his new group of young ensigns, just out of advanced flying school. He set out first to teach the veteran members of the squadron—Leppla, Vejtasa, Edwards and Faulkner—the intricacies of air combat when directed against Zeros or such other types of Japanese aircraft as they might meet in action.

Jim was fortunate in that these men, though experienced and tough air fighters, had never belonged to a fighter squadron and thus had no preconceived ideas or faults which needed to be erased. They approached this new type of fighting with open minds and took hold of the new technique rapidly. In double-quick time Flatley had four skilled section leaders and was ready to start spreading his doctrine and provide practical combat training for the still green men.

The four experienced scout pilots and Dave Pollock formed the nucleus upon which he built. Their years of flying and combat experience were valuable assets. When they took up a Wildcat for the first time in San Diego, they were thrilled by its power and control. They came down filled with the exhilaration which comes only from a first flight in a combat plane. Accustomed to the sluggishness of slower machines, the Wildcat seemed to them a super plane, and they would not listen to suggestions of the Zero's superiority. Flying their Dauntless SBDs they had exchanged shots with

Zeros, and after the feel of the Wildcat, they were firmly convinced that they would have little difficulty in handling the yellow monkeys. They were happy as children.

Jim had every reason to be pleased with their enthusiasm, but he never for an instant lost sight of the gap that was still to be bridged before they were ready.

Carrier fighters have three prime missions. They must prevent hostile bombers or torpedo planes from hitting their carrier; failure to do so might mean the loss of the carrier and expose accompanying warships to destruction. They must escort their own bombardment planes in their attack on hostile targets, but they must never let themselves be drawn away by hostile fighters, no matter how great the temptation. Finally, they must strafe enemy targets such as ships and land positions with bombs and machine guns. In this last mission the fighter is free of all restraint. Somewhere below lies his target. It cannot escape. It can hurl explosive shell and send up a hail of small projectiles, but it cannot maneuver around him nor shoot at him from close range. His only real danger is the defending enemy fighter plane. When he comes to blows with it the result is a straight duel between fighters. He has only himself to defend, which does not worry our fliers. They are confident of handling the Jap and welcome the chance to demonstrate it.

Although there is plenty of danger in ground strafing, it is generally considered "easier" than having to defend a sought-after target. During the instruction period Flatley constantly pointed out to his Reapers that the maneuvers in which they were being drilled so thoroughly were designed principally to provide defense against enemy fighters. Their formations, therefore, were vastly different from the fancy formations of peacetime flying exhibitions. The evolutions they had to practice until they could "fly them with their eyes shut" trained the boys to make attack runs again and again without losing the initial advantage. They were also taught to deliver attack after attack in a minimum of air space—a valuable asset when the pilot is forced to take on the enemy within a small area.

The weave employed by our fliers, in which the Reapers were rehearsed over and over until they became proficient, was developed by Thach, after whom it is named. Plenty of Japs have seen it in action.

To get the most out of a fighter plane's supply of ammunition, Flatley undertook painstakingly to teach his men everything the Navy knew about gunnery—and that was a great deal, because the Navy, years before, had learned how to transfer its lethal deadliness with deck weapons into the air.

In Europe the strategists had followed the easiest path and developed tactics which aimed to bring a plane in from astern, in an attack from above. The approach from right astern, or directly ahead, are the simplest shots. Our Navy had fostered and worked out deflection shooting, shooting at an angle, realizing that much time and opportunity is lost in trying to get astern of a maneuvering enemy, and that it would be practically impossible to attain such a position against a faster plane. In an approach from the side, at a right angle, for instance, the guns must be aimed a long distance ahead, owing to the high speed of the target. This makes it necessary to "lead" the target just as the hunter leads when he fires at a bird flying across his path.

In the approach, due allowance must be made not only for the relative positions of the planes, but also for their corresponding speed. If the approach is only a fraction late, the enemy has gone by before the attacker is within range. If the enemy is very fast, he will get away altogether.

Air gunnery, more than any other kind of gunnery, must reach the apex of exactitude and precision. It demands the kind of sound judgment displayed by Leppla on May 7 and 8, when he husbanded his ammunition and shot with such flawless perfection that he collected four Jap scalps one day and three the next. He might have been lost on the last day if he had not used his ammunition sparingly and aimed with such accuracy.

Butch O'Hare's performance in shooting down five and damaging the sixth of a nine-plane flight of enemy bombers well illustrates Thach's tactics. Butch attacked repeatedly without losing his selected position above and abeam of the enemy formation. He accounted for a plane every time he pressed the trigger, using no more bullets than were necessary. He fired only while his plane was flying "smooth." With extraordinary marksmanship, he brought down each plane with approximately forty rounds from each gun.

These were some of the things the Reapers set out to emulate. They trained hard and constantly to attain that perfection which would send them out a strong and hard-hitting fighting unit. They would show the Japs what stuff American men were made of—and they did.

Chapter 5

GUADALCANAL

Japanese fighting power was whittled down considerably at Midway. After that action, the enemy's carrier plane strength was reduced to the point where it could support no more than island hopping and overland drives, and protect supply lines to forward bases in the southwest Pacific and the Far Eastern enterprises.

Our western approach to the Pacific's eighty-million-odd square miles was temporarily quite safe from further assault. The approximate 7000-mile sea perimeter enclosing the Jap-occupied islands, which we formerly had to guard against surprise enemy jabs, was now cut down to the sea lane leading from Hawaii to Fiji, New Caledonia and New Guinea, instead of running from the Aleutians to New Guinea.

Our land-based air strength had been built up sufficiently to stave off any sea-air raids the enemy might attempt against Hawaii. Our new land route to Alaska and our forti-fied air arm in the Aleutians could be expected, with occa-sional aid from naval task forces, to stem enemy thrusts along the Aleutian-island land bridge. The need no longer existed to tie up a large part of our most powerful warships in the defense of the Hawaiian-Aleutian arc.

The sea-air engagements in the Coral Sea and Midway, the harassing raids in February on the Marshall and Gilbert Islands by Admiral Halsey, in March on Lae and Salamaua by Rear Admiral Brown, in April on Wake and Marcus, again by Halsey, and the Tokyo raid by Jimmie Doolittle's Army bombers flown off the *Hornet*—all these had been de-

fensive actions. Only now, after the battle of Midway, had
the Pacific war picture changed sufficiently to allow us to
switch from the defensive; only now were we in a position
to consider ways and means of rolling back the enemy. Midway was much more than a naval victory; it revised our
naval strategy.

The Japanese occupied every island in the northeastern
part of the Indian Ocean, and in the Pacific to the north of
Australia. Although American and Australian forces under
General Douglas MacArthur held the eastern end of the
southern New Guinea shore, Japan had all of the northern
and northeastern harbors of that 1700-mile-long island. The
enemy had also filtered down to the southeast through the
Solomons, the main islands of which are appreciable land
areas. The Japs controlled them more by sea-air domination
than by the number of soldiers based there.

When the Japs took over Guadalcanal they also occupied
and began to fortify Tulagi and the adjoining slopes of
Florida. They set an outpost on Savo, put a token force on
the rugged island of Malaita, eighty miles long and lying
thirty miles to the north of Guadalcanal, and they established air bases on Ysabel, Kolombangara and Bougainville.
For some reason they made no attempt to garrison the east-
ernmost island, San Cristobal, which is fifty-five miles long
and lies southeast of Guadalcanal.

Guadalcanal is about sixty miles long and thirty wide. An
undulating mountain range, with peaks as high as six thousand feet, follows the coast line roughly. Along the weather
side, or southern shore, the terrain is marshy. A winding
river, the Ithaca, links the swamps and drains them into the
sea. Exposure to the prevailing southerly winds and the
marshy nature of the ground left this side unoccupied by
planters. On the northern shore several great level flats between the foothills and the coast reach in some places almost

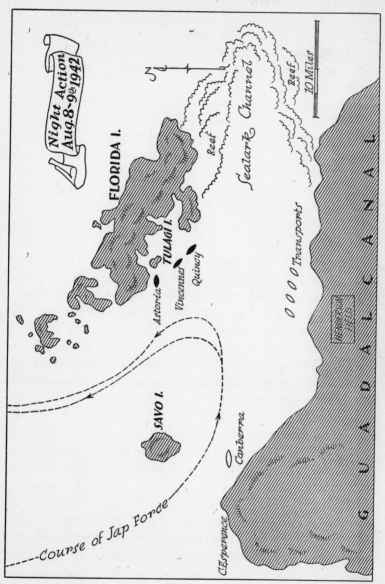

Night Action, August 8-9, 1942

to the ocean. These flat lands had been planted with coconut palms.

The Japs had chosen the grounds of a fine plantation for the construction of an airfield. After removing the palms they were able to build a broad, long landing strip on the best-drained area in the island.

Florida, across from Guadalcanal's north shore, is small and only about twelve miles wide. Sealark Channel, a 20-mile-wide sea lane, also known as Savo Sound, separates the two. Adjoining Florida is Tulagi Island, about two miles long. The bay formed by these two islands was known as Gavutu, but at present is more frequently referred to as Tulagi Harbor.

Interisland travel was in launches before the war. The village of Tulagi, off Florida, had the distinction of being the main center and "metropolis." It was the residence of the British commissioner and the headquarters of the district officers who maintained law and order in the islands. There were a rough, nine-hole golf course and a pair of tennis courts. The general store sold everything from floor rugs to whisky. Gala days were those two or three days every six weeks when the mainland (Australia) steamer came to Tulagi and everyone gathered for the occasion from all the islands, near and far.

At the western ingress to Sealark Channel lies Savo Island, a small upthrust. This speck is only about a mile across and stands directly between Cape Esperance, on Guadalcanal, and Tulagi. The channel's southern entrance, between Savo and Cape Esperance, is perhaps twelve miles and its northern entrance nine miles across. At its western entrances and well into the sound, the channel is deep, averaging between 300 and 500 fathoms (six feet to a fathom). The sound narrows toward its eastern exit because of coral shelves which come to within twenty or thirty feet of the surface, except for a passage no more than a mile wide which has a depth of 175 fathoms.

Inside the sound, on the northern shore of Guadalcanal, the splendid bomber and fighter landing strip was nearing completion. Finished, it would not only serve as an excellent air base, but it would furnish protection for fleet units in the fine anchorage of Savo Sound and Tulagi Harbor. Once bombers and fighters were based on this new airfield it would be easy for Japan to reach out eastward via San Cristobal to Santa Cruz and the New Hebrides, and further than that, to New Caledonia and the Fijis. Having come this far, the Japs would be free to send their ships into the southern Pacific to sever our lifeline to Australia. This airfield, therefore, had to be snatched from an enemy not yet fully accustomed to the new naval alignment in the Pacific, before it abounded with enemy air strength.

The main Japanese sea-air base was at Rabaul, in New Britain, but several smaller subsidiary air bases had been established on other islands of the New Guinea-Solomons group in the six months since the enemy had moved into the area. There were airfields on Lae, Salamaua, Kieta, Kavieng and Buna. Faisi and Rekata also possessed seaplane bases and gave shelter to warships and transports. The quiet waters of Tulagi based long-range, armed-patrol flying boats and seaplane fighters.

Our ship anchorages were in the Fijis, New Caledonia and Australia; our airfields were in the Fijis, New Hebrides, at Port Moresby, and along the northeast coast of Australia—entirely too far removed for land-based fighters to reach Guadalcanal and return without refueling. MacArthur's bombers alone were able to span the hops from Port Moresby to any of the enemy anchorages or flying fields through the New Guinea-Solomons area.

Japan had the important advantage of being able to cover

our bomber operations over Guadalcanal, and therefore to
oppose any bombardment planes that we could send in to
soften up the target. Consequently, it was essential that our
force invading Guadalcanal should include carriers. Marines,
assigned earlier to the defense of our South Pacific outposts,
were on hand to provide the initial landing force, and Army
units, disposed along Pacific posts, were in readiness to follow
them into Guadalcanal. The first bombardment would have
to be accomplished by carrier squadrons. After an occupation has been effected, fighter planes, flying in from the New
Hebrides, would free the carriers and enable them to swing
north or northwest to strike out at Japanese units coming
down from Rabaul or Truk. To coincide with the operation,
MacArthur's bombers would pound Jap air bases and ship-
ping heavily.

The plan was prepared and the campaign launched by
Rear Admiral Robert Lee Ghormley, in command of the
New Zealand zone; Vice Admiral Frank Fletcher, commanding the carrier task force; Rear Admiral R. K. Turner, respon-
sible for the transport and supply vessels carrying the invading force and equipment; and Major General Alexander A.
Vandegrift, senior officer of the Marines. General Mac-
Arthur's command extended from halfway between Australia
and New Zealand up to about the tenth parallel longitude,
through the lower Solomons—leaving Guadalcanal outside
his territory—and then turned north, where it included the
Philippines.

The Marines embarked aboard transports, escorted by
warships and several carriers, including the *Wasp* and *Enterprise,* and headed north until southeast of Guadalcanal,
where they swung toward the western end of that island.
Carrier air scouts, on the vigil for Japanese warships, ranged
ahead, and as far across the ocean as they could spread,
Navy fighters swept the skies to prevent long-range Jap patrol planes from getting through and spotting our transports.

As darkness closed down two American task forces were converging on Guadalcanal. The speeding *Wasp*, assigned to give air support for the venture, and her escort of cruisers and destroyers raced ahead, while the second force—transports carrying the Marines, the Coast Guardsmen who were to man the landing boats, the supplies of guns, tractors, equipment of all kinds and food—pressed on with its cruisers and destroyers, at the top speed of the slowest merchant vessel. A carefully calculated distance had to be covered.

Shortly after 2 A.M. on August 7, a leading destroyer, followed by cruisers and more destroyers, nosed around the western end of Guadalcanal and by three-thirty was guiding the column through the southern channel into Savo Sound. Here the force separated into two sections, one to take station off Tulagi on the north side of the sound, and the other to string out off Guadalcanal, on the southern end. The transports closed up. It was still too dark to make out any details on shore, but the Marines were straining for a look at the island. Only the dim shadows of the mountains were discernible.

There was bustling activity aboard the vessels. Windlasses lifted landing boats off the decks and lowered them into the water. As each was set down, its crew of Coast Guardsmen started the engine and followed astern. When the ships stopped, off their designated landing places, most of the barges had been launched and were waiting alongside for the Marines to board them for the trip ashore. The warships' guns pounded raucously against the defenses.

The *Wasp's* fighter squadron, led by Lieutenant Commander Courtney Shands, of Kirkwood, Missouri, and her scout bombers skippered by Lieutenant Commander Ernest M. Snowden, of Beaufort, North Carolina, droned overhead reassuringly. They had already accounted for a Kawanishi anchored at Tulagi, and for some fourteen Zero float-plane fighters. Some of the Zeros were destroyed on near-by

Gavutu, where they sat hauled up on a concrete landing ramp; the others were dealt with as they tried to take off.

While some of Snowden's scouts reconnoitered the surrounding seas, the remainder of his squadron teamed up with the dive bombers to attack enemy gun emplacements. The red streaks of their tracer bullets cut into the half-dark.

After the first shelling a few landing boats drew away from the transports and sped toward land. In them were Colonel LeRoy P. Hunt, USMC, and his Combat Group. They were to seize the beach and form the bridgehead through which the main force was to move.

Colonel Hunt and his men landed without a hitch. As the light grew stronger a few Japanese guns opened fire. Snowden's dive bombers silenced them with bombs. There was a surprising lack of enemy activity on Guadalcanal. The landing force scouted the area and sent up a flare to indicate there was no opposition. By 10 A.M. the first wave of our main force lighted on the island. Hour after hour the Coast Guard shuttled back and forth, each time returning with a boat load of Marines and supplies.

By 10:45, another combat group, led by Colonel C. B. Cates, had assembled on land and began to move to the southwest. It fanned out and pushed through the tall Kuni grass. The men left on the beach heard an occasional rifle report, sometimes from a Jap sniper, sometimes from the Marines who were shooting at suspicious movements ahead. There was no major contact with the retiring enemy. The terrain presented obstacles, and through the morning and early afternoon the advance was slow. Dense undergrowth and the many tributaries of the small Ilu River made progress difficult.

A Japanese bombing attack was to be expected, probably by noontime. It would take that long to organize an attack force from Rabaul. The arrival of enemy planes about 2 P.M. was the signal for our warships to turn their guns skyward, and as Jap bombers and fighters flew overhead amid bursts of anti-aircraft shells, our small Wildcats gave them a thorough going over. Horizontal bombers fell out of the sky, having accomplished little. A half hour later, a formation of dive bombers arrived. Their greater accuracy scored some hits, a square one on a destroyer and enough near misses to cause damage. A few of them were brought down.

Otherwise, the first day on Guadalcanal was quiet. Landing operations and the securing of the camp continued without interruption. Shortly after the air attack Marine headquarters established a command post among the coconut palms south of the east branch of the Ilu River.

But the story on Tulagi was far different.

This small island had been heavily fortified and well armed by the enemy. The main Jap stronghold was in the steep, excavated sides of a hill on the southeast end of Tulagi. Caves and generous dugouts were used as machine-gun and mortar positions. All were interconnected in groups and each group had communication with the others by radio. The general plan followed by the enemy was to have positions which covered all open low ground.

At 7 A.M. the Marines disembarked. Their barges lined up in the assembly area (a space between two destroyers to mark the jumping-off line), where some of the new landing boats had gathered already. These boats were strong steel hulls fitted with a ramp at the bow, which could be lowered to enable men, tanks and guns to be rushed ashore once the shallow-draft vessel ground to a stop. Amphibious tractors fitted with wheel treads, acting as paddlewheels to drive them through the water, also made ready to land.

The destroyers had cleared the way by sharp, brisk shelling. Now they lifted their fire to pump projectiles into the ridges close inland. The first boats rubbed their prows onto the beach and the Marines leaped ashore.

Brigadier General William H. Rupertus, assistant commander of the invading troops, personally directed the operations on Tulagi and later described the battle as "the most wonderful work we have had in history."

Captain E. J. Crane landed with his company on the west side of the promontory on Florida, which overlooks Tulagi Island. He met with no opposition.

The first wave of Raiders, led by Colonel Merritt Edison, approached a beach to the northwest of Tulagi. They had expected strong resistance, but to their surprise scarcely a shot was fired. The Japs evidently had not expected a landing to be attempted at this point. Many well-defined trails led along the beach at the base of a ridge running to the southeast, but the Raiders ignored this opportunity. Instead, they climbed the hogback. They found it extremely rugged going. After two hours they had progressed only one and a half miles.

At this point they approached a cross ridge. Here they ran into their first stiff resistance. The Japs, hidden along the hillside, covered the Raiders with deadly machine-gun and rifle fire.

The Marines pressed closer, breaking up into small parties. As each enemy nest was located, they circumambulated cautiously, with an eye on the enemy-occupied cave, and crawled to positions on the steep hillside from which they could lob hand grenades into the cliff holes. Each nest had to be attacked individually. It was dangerous work.

A second Marine company pushed through strong opposition on the north side of Tulagi and captured a ridge overlooking the Japs' recreation field. From concealed positions in trees, behind buildings and large boulders, the Japs opened and sustained fire on their rear.

By this time Captain Harold T. A. Richmond, who had come ashore at the north end, was leading his company southward. He, too, ran into heavy machine-gun fire from ravine strong posts.

It was now almost dark. The Raiders organized a defensive position for the night. It was decided to form the lines to the northwest of the hill, fronting on Captain Richmond's force.

The night was anything but quiet. The Japanese launched a fierce counterattack at 10:30 P.M. They crept up close, then charged. A deadly hand-to-hand fight raged in the inky darkness. They fought with knives, grenades and rifles, exerting sufficient pressure on one point to break through between two of our companies, isolating one. They continued to drive northward and flowed toward the British Residency to the north of the playing field.

There a small band of Marines, eight men under Lieutenant John E. Doyle, earned their military immortality. They formed a mortar observation post. When the Japs reached Doyle's position he and his men pushed the enemy back, driving them over a low precipice on his flank.

Next morning, in the graying dawn, the two companies which had mopped up the northern end of Tulagi the day before attacked and forced the Japs to the south. Simultaneously a third company broke through from the west, and by noon the enemy was surrounded on three sides and driven to bay in the fortified hill. Before night fell the Japs were blasted out. Isolated groups hid in trees, gorges and caves. Ceaselessly the Marines combed the island until they were uprooted. None surrendered.

While this battle raged on Tulagi, the main landing force on Guadalcanal had a comparatively easy task. It followed a westerly direction until it reached and occupied the airfield.

Continuing to the Lunga River in the north central part, defense works were erected on Lunga Point and other areas to protect the flying field. There was no resistance until the combat groups neared Kukum, a tiny native village consisting of a handful of huts. It was disposed of quickly.

The enemy had evacuated the camps around the new airfield in a hurry, leaving great stores of rice, beer and other supplies behind. Mess kits were found, some half full of an unfinished meal. Ammunition, guns, fuel for tractors and planes, trucks, cars, refrigerating machinery, road rollers, an electric power plant and personal gear were strewn about, undestroyed.

Jap bombers returned at midday, about forty of them, to attack our transports. Many of them were shot down. A burning bomber crashed into the forward hold of the *George F. Elliott,* formerly the old Baltimore Mail Steamship Company's *Los Angeles.* The subsequent fire destroyed this vessel. There was no other damage.

On Gavutu our forces attacked and won a footing. In the center of this small, mile-long island, a 148-foot hill overlooks the flats adjoining the beaches. The enemy had converted this hill into a miniature Gibraltar. Great caverns, about twenty feet by twenty feet, had been hewn into the rock. Several were connected by passages carved into the cragged hill.

On the beach the Japanese had built concrete seaplane ramps on which the attacking party intended to land. As they approached, it became apparent that the morning's naval bombardment had shattered the concrete and tossed great blocks of it into the water, making it impossible to bring the landing barges inshore.

Undeterred, the Marines made for a high wharf and clambered up it. They came under heavy machine-gun fire directed from the hill overlooking the beach. Their commanding officer, Major Robert H. Williams, who led the first wave, was badly wounded. Captain George Stallings immediately took over and proceeded to ferret the enemy out of his fortifications.

On this small island one of the most sanguinary engagements of the entire action was fought. The Marines had expected to have to deal with perhaps a hundred of the enemy.

Actually, there were 450 Japs. By the evening of August 8, 448 of them were buried and two were held captive.

Captain Harry L. Torgerson played a large part in hunting them out. Four of his men covered him with their rifles while he wormed his way about on the face of the hilly fortress. With them they carried a large supply of TNT charges attached to boards. From selected vantage points, he would toss the handmade stick bombs into the mouths of the caverns. Falling boulders and debris would do the rest. He sealed more than fifty caves and suffered only the loss of a wristwatch and the indignity of having his pants torn off.

The assault on Tanambogo, only five hundred yards off Gavutu and connected with it by a causeway, turned into another small but desperate action for a handful of Marines. This island, too, was strongly held by an enemy prepared to fight to the last. Captain Crane, who had brought his company ashore on Florida without opposition earlier in the action, was ordered at 2 P.M. on August 7 to push on to Tanambogo. Heavy machine-gun fire prevented the Marines from crossing the causeway, so the island had to be taken by direct assault.

Flight Lieutenant C. E. Spencer, of the Royal Australian Air Force, acted as guide. The men embarked late in the afternoon to force a landing at dusk. As they advanced, American warships moved in to bombard the beach and back areas in an attempt to bring out the defenders. As the Marines felt their way shoreward an unlucky shell set fire to a big oil dump near the beach. Bright gasoline flames illuminated the approaching force, subjecting it to extremely heavy machine-gun fire. The flame also disclosed that the enemy had built a second high jetty extending from the small beach. Unexpectedly the landing boats found themselves packed between the two piers. They withdrew and delayed the attack until dawn.

Next morning two light tanks were brought to Gavutu

to be sent across the causeway. Lieutenant Colonel R. G. Hunt directed the assault. The tanks crossed safely, but after the leading tank had progressed about a hundred feet inland, Japs swarmed out of their holes, disabled it by jamming iron bars into its bogies, poured gasoline over it and set it afire.

Melting heat forced the crew to abandon the vehicle. The commanding lieutenant opened the turret, took over the all-purpose machine gun mounted there and killed twenty-three Japanese before they stabbed him to death. Meanwhile, the Marine infantry had crossed over and mopped up the enemy garrison, avenging their comrade's death.

The "know-how" of our combined forces had thus won us all our objectives within the first forty-eight hours.

Near the evening of August 8 a scout plane reported a powerful enemy fleet, including battleships, headed for Savo Sound. The enemy's position, course and speed indicated the force would arrive by about 2 A.M.

Precisely at two a lone plane flew slowly over the American warships, dropping flares. Even as they burst into flame a searchlight flared up on near-by Savo, adding to the illumination. To the enemy ships, obscured in the night, our warships presented a brilliant target.

For fifteen minutes the Japs showered them with hails of explosives and torpedoes. The shells began to hit even while "battle stations" sounded. The enemy came in, steamed around Savo Island and headed right back out to sea.

Our damage was heavy. We lost four cruisers of 10,000 tons with 8-inch guns: the *Astoria, Quincy, Vincennes* and the Australian cruiser *Canberra*. Why the Japanese withdrew without attacking our transports and other escort vessels is difficult to say.

After the transports finished unloading, all the ships. including the aircraft carrier *Wasp*, hauled out and returned to a rear operational base. They had brought temporary relief. In the following weeks, however, our position on Guadalcanal grew more and more precarious. There was only inadequate equipment with which to repulse the almost constant Japanese air and sea attacks, and an inadequate number of ground troops and airmen.

The arrival of Major John L. Smith and his Marine fighter squadron somewhat alleviated the situation. They gave the island its first fighter plane defense and took toll of the Japs day after day. But the problem of supplies and reinforcements had still to be solved if we were to continue to make progress, or even to retain control of the gains already made. On the 1500-odd square miles of Guadalcanal, of which we held only about fifteen, Japan was building up a strong garrison.

It became vital to bring the enemy to battle, and in circumstances satisfactory to ourselves. We had to interrupt the Japs' flow of reinforcements and divert the naval forces which prevented us from augmenting our foothold on the island.

At the end of the third week in August, two weeks after the invasion of Guadalcanal, a powerful American carrier task force was dispatched to the northeastern Solomons. In co-operation with General MacArthur's land-based bombers, who reconnoitered the entire Solomons area from Port Moresby, we administered a blow to Japanese naval power and plans.

Advised by Fortresses of the location of two enemy carriers, a battleship, cruisers, destroyers and transport vessels, our carrier force closed in. Fighting 6, commanded by Lieutenant L. H. Bauer, made the first contact. Leading four Wildcats, Ensign Doyle C. Barnes intercepted a float-plane, the vanguard of the Jap air group, and downed this Jap in the first pass. Then Fighting 6 awaited the swarm.

Two formations of Aichi 99s (dive bombers), eighteen in

each formation, came in at 20,000 feet. Lieutenant A. O. Vorse, Jr., taking his four-plane fighter section up to defend his carrier, ran into the first Zeros at 8000 feet. A hot fight ensued. Vorse fought defensively and climbed. At 20,000 feet the Zeros pulled off. Vorse had never lost sight of the Aichis meanwhile. They were well below now, in a full power glide and ready for the turnover. Vorse led his section down. Another group of Zeros intercepted as the Wildcats reached the 12,000-foot level, and Vorse had a real fight on his hands. Ensign F. R. Register came to the rescue and scored a hit on a Zero; the Jap pilot fairly popped out of his cockpit, without a parachute. Vorse, too, scored a kill. As Register pulled back toward his flight a Jap Messerschmitt 109 flashed past. Again Register fired and sent this copy of the German fighter down in flames. Machinist D. E. Runyon, of Waynetown, Indiana, bagged three Aichis during this air fight. In all, the sixteen airmen accounted for twenty-eight Jap planes.

The Fortresses claimed four bomb hits on a large enemy flat-top. Navy dive bombers and torpedo planes scored hits on the small 7100-ton carrier *Ryuzyo* and, within forty-eight hours, bombed a battleship, several cruisers, one destroyer, one transport and four miscellaneous craft. The action comprised scattered onslaughts during which one American carrier was subjected to a powerful attack by Japanese bombers and torpedo planes in the late afternoon of August 24.

Although these raids failed to achieve any spectacular success, the appearance of American forces disturbed and delayed the enemy's program enough to keep the Japs from getting supplies and reinforcements through on schedule. Further, it prevented them from overwhelming our small, beleaguered force during the first critical weeks and gave us some much-needed time in which to strengthen and fortify our own small gains.

Chapter 6

ENEMY BOUND

In EARLY August the Reapers left San Diego for Hawaii to complete their flight training. They were assigned station and quarters on a Navy airfield at Oahu, where they received their final polish.

Their stay in the Hawaiians was made particularly pleasant by Alexa von Temsky Zabrieski, an artist, who kept her beautiful home on the slopes of Hale Akala on Maui, the Valley Isle, open to the fliers. Her house was perched on the side of a steep hill and commanded a wide view across valley and ocean. Alexa had been born and raised in Hawaii, where her father settled after he fought the Maoris in New Zealand. With the outbreak of war, she concentrated her energies on the fliers stationed on the airfield and threw her place open to them. Whenever training schedules permitted, they would take advantage of her standing invitation and while away their off hours.

At her table could be found whatever luxuries were still available in the islands, and to keep her larder well stocked, the airmen hunted pheasants and other game birds on the soft slopes of the surrounding hills. There were riding horses at their disposal, and there was always swimming. Her sole concern was to see the men comfortable and nothing pleased her so much as to know they felt at home.

Intuitive Alexa never failed to sense the little anxieties and worries which troubled her adopted sons and always managed to find the right words to assuage their private fears and griefs. She showed great sympathy for those who were homesick and lent a patient ear to those who needed her compassion. Commander Flatley declared: "She was a one-woman USO, and more besides."

She urged the boys to write home often and frequently took up the pen herself to post personal notes to wives and mothers. When the Reapers were finally ready to go to battle she gave them a farewell party and planned for their return. She corresponded with the squadron through their months of absence, and at Christmas, wrote that their presents were waiting. She asked Jimmy Flatley to sit for his portrait, with which she surprised Mrs. Flatley at Christmas, as she had surprised Mrs. Ramsey before her with a painting of Paul Ramsey, commander of an Air Group. Her hospitality, friendship and the homelike atmosphere she created gave the Reapers something they feel they can never repay.

Captain John Murphy, commander of the small naval flying field, was another person to whom the Reapers feel indebted. He gave them every possible aid in their final weeks of preparation and leaned over backward to see that they had every help in their training program.

At Oahu the Reapers acquired some additional and experienced pilots. Lieutenant H. S. Packard of Fighting 2, who had fought in the Battle of the Coral Sea and come out of it with an excellent record, asked to be taken in. So did Lieutenant Gordon Fierbaugh, just back from in and around Guadalcanal, where he had fought from a carrier, downed three Japs in the early invasion, and was forced to parachute into the sea. Bailing out of his wrecked plane, he was injured but saved himself by swimming for five hours to shore. Since then he had been under medical care. Flatley wanted to have him in the squadron if the Navy doctor said yes. Final X-rays disclosed that he still suffered from several fractured vertebrae and Jim, reluctantly, had to give up all thought of including Fierbaugh. Gordon's desire to get back into the fight, in spite of his injuries, had a profound effect on the young Reapers. They felt proud and privileged to be members of a squadron which combat men like Packard and Fierbaugh wanted to join.

Then there was Lieutenant Commander W. R. Kane, a friend of Flatley's. An experienced fighter pilot, he held a staff office job in Hawaii and wanted, more than anything else, to change over to the Reapers.

One evening, in the company of Captain Miles Browning, chief of staff to Admiral Halsey, Kane put in his plea. Browning, a man of sound judgment and a flier and active pilot for more than twenty years, understood only too well what motivated Kane's request. He informed him the following day that permission had been granted. "Killer" Kane, thus transferred, became executive officer of the Reapers.

Before sailing orders arrived, one more volunteer joined the group. Lieutenant Stanley E. Ruehlow, who had been through Midway as a member of Fighting 8, companion squadron to expended Torpedo 8, had got lost and eventually his Wildcat ran out of gasoline. He set his plane into the sea and spent five days in his tiny rubber boat, tossing about the ocean, until a Catalina found and rescued him. Recuperating in Hawaii from his ordeal, he spent much time with the Reapers. Constant contact with them, and hearing about their plans and preparations, made him want to get back into the fight with them. They were only too happy to have him.

By this time the squadron had assembled enough Wildcats to provide each flier with a machine. None were new and many were well used. The mechanics and armorers were kept busy bringing these aircraft up to fighting pitch. But they were soundly constructed and well designed, and after a general overhaul, tune-up and furbishing job, they were once more excellent, reliable combat weapons when the ground crews were finished.

"Nut splitters," as they are frequently referred to, are the pilot's most trusted friends. He relies on them and depends on them to keep his plane flying. For the ground crew, there is none of the excitement of diving, zooming and shooting at enemy machines. They send their pilots off with fingers crossed and are on the jump when the boys bounce back aboard. Lightninglike, they refuel and rearm the planes, and in no time have them off again and in the fight. Once the mechanic says, "She's O.K.," and the plane takes off, the pilot's fate rests to a considerable extent on how well the ground crew has done its job. He never doubts that the job has been well done.

Until recently, individual squadrons had their own ground crews who traveled and moved about with them. They shared the squadron's exuberance when operations were concluded successfully and turned somber with the rest at misfortune or loss. Today, squadrons are separate entities, divorced from mechanics and armorers, and the latter have become part of the carrier's crew and remain aboard like gunners and the black gang. It is probably a better plan, but ground crews will miss the closer and more intimate association.

Announcement of the loss of the carrier *Wasp* struck like a lightning bolt before the Reapers left Hawaii. The carrier was returning to an advanced base on September 15 when, at approximately 3 P.M., without warning, three torpedoes from a Jap sub in ambush exploded in the vicinity of her magazines and gasoline tanks.

The blasts ripped great holes in her plates and set fires which grew in intensity in spite of the efforts of her crew. About fifteen minutes later a second, greater explosion rocked her hull, spreading the fire throughout the ship. She remained afloat for about five more hours. Ninety per cent of her crew was rescued.

The *Wasp* was one of our newest carriers, and the only one lost to us other than in battle. She had been completed and brought into commission in 1940, and although she carried four squadrons, or as many planes as the *Enterprise* (20,000 tons) and *Saratoga* (33,000 tons), she displaced only 14,700 tons. She was launched under ominous war clouds and was the sixth naval vessel to bear that name. After a brief shakedown cruise, she carried a formation of P-40s (Curtiss Warhawks) to Iceland, then turned up at Scapa Flow in the spring of 1942, and from there she proceeded to the besieged Mediterranean island of Malta, with an urgently needed load of planes.

A second time she returned from Scapa Flow with a second cargo of aircraft. This time she drew near the embattled little bastion during a German air attack. Her Spitfires took off and literally tore into the Luftwaffe from out of the blue.

In Scapa Flow a third time, the *Wasp* was welcomed back by Winston Churchill's succinct message; "Who says a *Wasp* can't sting twice?"

Early in October the Reapers received orders to report aboard the *Enterprise,* "the fightingest ship in the United States Navy." The mighty carrier was commanded by Captain A. C. Davis, later by Captain O. B. Hardison. The air officer was Commander John Crommelin, past master of the inverted spin, who in demonstrations at naval flying schools had illustrated to fledgling airmen how to extricate themselves safely from this deadliest of spins. He was an excellent morale builder.

The squadron's gear was put aboard and the crew members moved on the carrier with their spares, tools and other equipment, and began to prepare for the arrival of the planes.

One morning the carrier released the lines and springs which held her alongside the pier at Pearl Harbor, backed into the basin, swung slowly, and headed through the channel. For the umpteenth time in this war she was returning to the battle zone.

On their field the Reapers waited nervously. They were to have an air exercise. They were to work out a problem in co-operation with the scouts, bombers and torpedo planes. All of the squadrons were new, and all had been built around a handful of battle-experienced fliers. Every man was excited and eager to embark on the mission. Even the more experienced men were filled with a tingling anticipation.

By midafternoon the carrier was many hours at sea and the squadrons were ready to find, practice attack, and report aboard. The problem of finding the ship fell to Scouting 10. The squadron ranged the sea, located and reported the position correctly. Navigation brought the other squadrons to their target.

They deployed for the attack exercise. The torpedo planes came, slanting down, the dive bombers peeled off and the fighters (the Reapers), acting as escort for all, maintained small sections of Wildcats above each group. Everything went according to plan.

The ships trained their guns at the circling, diving and maneuvering planes, gun sights following their flight. The gunnery department—range finders, target locators, talkers—went through the motions in "dry runs." These drills are just as important as actual shooting at moving targets. They serve to iron out all kinds of kinks.

For many of the gunners this was their first voyage out. It is the custom to include on every ship a crew about 20 per cent of which is on its first and 20 per cent on its second cruise. This system has supplied successfully the vast number of men we need at sea, without lessening any ship's fighting efficiency. The newer men are welded smoothly with the old and thus become part of the fleet without special effort.

Late afternoon saw all the squadrons aboard and secured. The mock fight was over. Old friendships were renewed among officers and men who had been together at sea or at shore bases. New acquaintances were made, and the younger Reapers for the first time walked the decks of a warship as members of its crew. The steel side bulkheads, the deck underfoot and the steel plates above had become their home. Hundreds of men they had never laid eyes on before were their shipmates. They would fight side by side, be dependent on each other, share much the same fate, and work toward one cause. They had joined a gigantic club, entrance into which, though selective, demands neither sponsor nor fee. Physical attributes and personal achievement were acceptable. Study and hard work had earned them full membership and trust, and the responsibility of fighting aboard an American warship.

The task force threaded its way along the island-dotted Pacific. Every daylight hour the carrier's squadrons were engaged in offensive and defensive maneuvers, and in practice aerobatics. The voyage was uneventful and the routine was much the same. For the Reapers, it meant instruction, flying and perhaps a game of checkers, chess, bridge or the old Navy stand-by, acey-deucy.

There was a short-lived flutter of excitement when a distant scout located some small Japanese ships one morning near an island in the lower Ellice group, but a couple of destroyers were sent off to deal with them, dashing the hopes of the eager young fliers. Reports brought in later established the sinking of two enemy patrol vessels and the damaging of one enemy destroyer and a merchant ship. (Shortly after, the United States moved into the most important islands of the Ellice group, where we now have an air base at Funafuti.)

Ball games were the favorite outdoor pastime. They were played on Fly 1, the wide flight deck forward which was usually kept clear so that aircraft could be launched without delay in an emergency.

On the afternoon of October 21 the Reapers had a session of Bull in the Ring, stripped of all except their skivvies. Forming a circle, with one man in the center as the bull, they threw a large ball back and forth among the players.

The bull tried to touch it in flight, which would release him from the center and make one of the outside men change places with him. There is much healthy exercise in the game, and it provides variety to an otherwise monotonous tossing of the medicine ball.

On this particular afternoon Reaper W. K. ("Bill") Blair, the bull, was throwing his 220-pound frame around, trying to catch the ball. When it was thrown to Jim Flatley he bounced and caught it, but as he landed back on his feet and braced himself for a quick lob, Bill fell against him with his full weight and smashed down on Jim's right foot. An examination showed that Jim had broken a small bone in the top of his instep. Although a doctor repaired the damage at once, Jim limped around the ship for three weeks. It handicapped him somewhat but did not keep him from his duties.

Three days later, on October 24, the *Enterprise* rendezvoused with the *Hornet*, a big new 35,000-ton battleship, and with several cruisers and destroyers. All these ships had been constructed for modern war and could do better than twenty-five knots. Durability and endurance had been built into every hull, along with speed, fire power and maneuverability. The ships were the finest of their class. As the Reapers gazed across the sea and calculated the power of each vessel, a new pride surged through them. Completely confident, they watched the whole force turn and head north—enemy bound.

Chapter 7

THE BATTLE OF CAPE ESPERANCE

OCTOBER began and our position on Guadalcanal was still desperate. Japanese naval superiority in the Solomons prevented us from getting more than a thin trickle of men through, only the most vital ammunition and barely sufficient gasoline to keep our few planes in the air. For sustenance, our force relied mainly on food captured from the enemy during the initial landing.

The same troops who had occupied the narrow three-by-five-mile strip along the beach seven weeks earlier were still in the front lines. We needed at least a division of fresh troops to relieve our exhausted fighters and another fresh division properly equipped and supplied to drive the Japanese from the area.

Despite the Japs' superior strategic position, we would have to match and overcome the enemy at sea and retard his flow of troops and supplies. Somehow we would have to base a strong force of bombardment planes on Henderson Field, with the necessary gasoline, bombs, torpedoes and machine-gun ammunition for offensive action.

Our campaign, originally aimed to snatch Guadalcanal from the Japanese, had developed from a local skirmish into a major test of sea power. It had developed into a serious struggle between the United States Navy and the Japanese Navy for control of the surrounding ocean. We had stuck our necks out, and the Japanese held the ax poised.

During late August and through the month of September, we had employed carrier task forces in and around the Solomons to strike at enemy convoys, air bases and warships. But Japan had several airfields available in the islands and she sent land-based planes against our flat-tops before they could get within range of enemy bases and accomplish their missions. We possessed far too few of these vital ships to risk them in uneven fight. We had to limit their use to forays and could not let them remain long enough in one area to interrupt seriously the enemy's ever-broadening stream of men and goods to his sector of Guadalcanal.

The "Tokyo Express" had been allowed to run on schedule too long. Regularly the transports, escorted by cruisers and destroyers, had set out from Rabaul and made their approach through the passage that lay between the New Georgia group and Santa Isabel. In this sheltered "slot" they were protected in daylight by fighter planes from their string of bases. At nightfall, under cover of darkness, they would steam their last lap to Guadalcanal, land, unload their cargo hurriedly and pull away again before dawn. Meanwhile, their escorting warships would steam into Savo Sound, shell our airfield, wreck parked planes, destroy gasoline dumps and harass our men generally. Their routine seldom varied.

With sufficient numbers of dive bombers, torpedo planes and escort fighters, we could probably have stopped their daylight runs, but the scant number of aircraft at our disposal gave us no chance.

The task of organizing a surface ship force to stop the Jap reinforcements and get our vessels through the enemy's naval blockade was assigned to Rear Admiral Norman Scott. A fifty-three-year-old Missourian, and "all Navy," he gathered around him a tight force of cruisers and destroyers, including the two 8-inch gun cruisers *San Francisco* and *Salt Lake City,* and the two modern cruisers *Boise* and *Helena.* By the end of the first week in October he was off in the direction of Guadalcanal. His flagship, the *San Francisco,* was manned by a crew whipped into fighting trim during many weeks at sea. Even though they had taken part in sea-air engagements during the previous ten months, the crewmen itched for a chance to exchange shots with Jap warships. Thus far their opportunity to get at the enemy had been limited mostly to shooting at hostile planes.

The *San Francisco*, of the same class as the lost *Astoria*, was commissioned in 1934, rated at 9950 tons, with a speed of 32.7 knots, and she was well armored. Her main batteries mounted nine 8-inch guns in three triple turrets and eight 5-inch guns, in addition to many smaller automatics as secondary all-purpose weapons.

The *Salt Lake City*, or "*Swayback Maru*," as she was named by the jovial correspondent Robert Casey in his *Torpedo Junction*, had already gained distinction in earlier Pacific actions. She and the *Pensacola* were sister ships, the only two of their class, and were completed in 1929. Her tonnage is given as 9100 and her speed as 32.7 knots. She was gunned with ten 8-inch rifles, 5-inch all-purpose weapons and the usual cluster of lighter automatics.

The *Boise* and *Helena*, of the *St. Louis* class, modern cruisers in every respect, had been commissioned as late as 1939. They were a new departure, as cruisers go, in mounting fifteen 6-inch guns in five triple turrets, three forward and two aft. Their secondary armament consisted of eight 5-inch all-purpose guns. These ships reportedly had been built to match the Japanese *Mogami* class, originally thought to be 8500 tons, armed with fifteen 6.1-inch guns. More recent reports, however, suggested that the Nips armed the *Mogamis* with 8-inch guns and built them considerably heavier than their reported tonnage. Another innovation introduced on the new United States cruisers was the housing of planes in a hangar built into the stern section of the main hull. To obtain the additional space for the planes below deck, the after end was built square, like a speedboat, instead of being shrunk, as are orthodox ships. The numerous smaller automatics, for defense against close aircraft, bristled all over their decks. These guns make every American warship a veritable pincushion of light defensive weapons.

The modern 8-inch, 6-inch and 5-inch guns, equipped with new rapid-operating breeches and up-to-the-minute loading mechanisms, have stepped up the rate of fire of our warships substantially. In the hands of experienced gunners these weapons allow each ship to pour out a maximum hail of destruction. Inasmuch as every warship is merely a self-propelled, armored, maneuverable platform to carry guns, the stepping up of the rate of fire is of utmost importance. This is induced by daily practice with dummy loaders, into which the projectile and driving charge is loaded, the breech closed and the gun "fired," until the greatest possible speed has been attained.

The 8-inchers' 250-pound armor-piercing projectiles have an initial muzzle velocity of 3000 feet per second. The 6-inchers hurl a 105 pound projectile at a very fast rate of fire.

Our 5-inch all-purpose weapons, the main armament of our destroyers, hurl a 51-pound shell that will penetrate 3.5 inches at 3000 yards. They have a devastating effect on superstructures, possess an extremely rapid rate of fire, and are semiautomatic. When the gun recoils, it ejects the empty brass cartridge case and the breech remains open while the loader packs it with the next cartridge and shell, which is a single unit. A second crew member snaps a lever which actuates the air pressure that closes the breech block and rams the shell home. The gun pointer keeps the sights on the target and the weapon is again ready to be fired. Ten to twelve rounds of these 51-pound missiles can be fired each minute, which is a superior performance.

With his hand-picked force, Admiral Scott cruised south of Guadalcanal, out of sight of enemy lookouts on mountain peaks and hidden from hostile planes. From there his ships could, unseen, make the run into Savo Sound during the first few hours of darkness, if necessary.

On October 9, Marine fliers had attacked Jap cruisers, destroyers and transports in the "slot." A dive-bombed cruiser was left down at the bow, minor damage was inflicted on a second cruiser and three Zero float-plane fighters which tried to interfere were shot down. Two days later our air scouts again reported a hostile force coming through the "slot." They were transports, escorted by three 8-inch gun cruisers, one 6-inch gun cruiser and six destroyers. Their course and speed indicated they would arrive off Savo about midnight.

This was the word for which Admiral Scott had been waiting. At dusk he would take his force up to intercept the enemy. His task was no sinecure. Three of the enemy cruisers had been identified. There was one of the *Nati* class, 10,000 tons, ten 8-inch guns mounted in five turrets, three forward and two aft, and eight torpedo tubes; one of the *Atago* class, 9850 tons, ten 8-inch guns mounted similarly, and eight torpedo tubes; and one of the *Kako* class, 7100 tons, with six 8-inch guns and a dozen torpedo tubes. The usual 4.7-inch all-purpose guns of their secondary batteries were distributed throughout the ships.

A daylight engagement would boil down to a contest between the Jap twenty-six rifles of 8-inch caliber and the 8-inch weapons of Admiral Scott's force, with the *Boise's* 6-inch rifles in a secondary role. Such an engagement would be fought at ranges outside the reach of the smaller weapons, and the use of torpedo tubes would be generally nullified, unless one side or the other sent destroyers in to deliver an attack. The outcome would be in ratio to the excellence of the gunnery department of each ship, the range-finding equipment, laying devices, skill of the personnel and the quality of the ordnance.

The action contemplated, however, would be fought at night and at extremely close range, where every gun, includ-

ing the secondaries, would be effective and in which torpedoes could be expected to run thick through the blacked-
out waters. Even poor gunnery might find targets, and as
for torpedoes, to stay out of their way would be pure luck.

Shortly before midnight the spotters reported contact with
hostile warships. The American force was in the sound, par-
alleling Guadalcanal's northern shore off Cape Esperance.
There was no need to call "quarters"; the ships' crews were
already standing to. In sonorous monotone the range finder
droned range and bearing of the enemy's ships.

The *San Francisco,* the *Helena,* the *Boise,* and the *Salt
Lake City* had just completed a turn. Our destroyers were
screening the cruisers against the enemy.

Finally the admiral gave the order to fire and all the
vessels erupted darting tongues of flame simultaneously.
After the first deafening salvo the guns operated indepen-
dently, as fast as the eager gun crews could reload, aim
and fire.

Flare shells thrown up by our force brought out the enemy
ships in sharp relief. These shells are aimed high and their
fuses are timed to burst a small powder charge, for the
purpose of rupturing the case. This frees a parachute.
Attached to the parachute is a magnesium or calcium com-
pound which burns fiercely. Its brilliant light illuminates a
wide area as the parachute drifts slowly down. Shooting
these flares beyond enemy ships silhouettes them and provides a perfect target.

With the enemy still unsettled, Admiral Scott's force took
full advantage of the general confusion. Our ships spread
their guns over several of the vessels, setting three of them
ablaze. There were a few retaliating shells as the enemy
gunners recovered and went into action. Then our destroyers
raced in close and unleashed their deadly torpedoes as the
Jap ships strove to take up their new disposition. Hits were
scored on two cruisers. One of the *Kako* class was sunk and

another damaged. The Japs, subjected to a continuous stream of projectiles, were not allowed to recover.

During the opening phase of the engagement, the *Boise*, commanded by Captain E. J. ("Mike") Moran, was putting on a grand show. The voices of her spotters over the communicators yelled with satisfaction every time another Jap began to burn and break up. The *Boise*, engaged with several Jap vessels, took only three hits during the first ten minutes. Her 5-inch guns were pounding at an enemy destroyer and her 6-inch rifles returning the fire of an 8-inch gun cruiser when the *Salt Lake City*, having finished off an auxiliary ship, moved her 8-inchers over to help the *Boise* with the heavy Jap. Their combined battering set the enemy ship afire. The flagship was lashing at Jap vessels one after the other and the *Helena* was squirting Jap destroyers and cruisers.

After ten minutes of fast steaming, maneuvering and slugging away at the enemy, Admiral Scott realigned his force and set it on a new course designed to close the range.

The *Boise*, now across from the enemy ships that survived the early phase of the attack, was brought under direct fire from the third heavy cruiser. Only three or four miles distant, the cruiser began to strike the *Boise* while she was engrossed in battle with another enemy vessel. Before she could switch her guns, the Jap's 8-inchers knocked out two of her three forward turrets and put a hole in her below the water line. Fires started near her forward magazines and were fed on the powder charges. Soon the flames were licking mast-high, drawing to the *Boise* the concentrated fire of all enemy vessels within range. Her captain, who had fought his ship in dashing style, feared an explosion below decks and was forced to swing to port, away from the enemy and out of the line. Even with all her forward section engulfed by flame, the *Boise's* after turrets continued to spit fire.

The gallant *Salt Lake City*, commanded by Captain Ernest G. Small, forged ahead to interpose herself between the stricken *Boise* and her main enemy. She took three heavy salvos within the first couple of minutes. The Japs were shooting well. Then the "Swayback Maru" pitched in, ultimately spoiling the Japs' aim.

This second phase of the battle had lasted only a few minutes, but it had been hot and fast. The scene had been one of great smoke clouds fogging the night's blackness, and of glowing, fire-gutted ships. Range had been anywhere from 1500 yards (against destroyers which attacked with torpedoes) to 5000 and 7500 yards between the heavy cruisers. At these ranges, all weapons were destructive. Never before in naval warfare had vessels been ripped and torn by such an incessant hail of explosive shell.

Under cover of smoke and darkness, destroyers from both forces had slid in close to discharge their torpedoes. They had fired at each other at point-blank range and faced the heavy guns of cruisers pointed at them at little more than a thousand yards. One American destroyer, the *Duncan,* was lost. She took her death blow while handing out torpedoes. Her gallant crew fought a losing battle during the night and following forenoon, trying to quench her fires and shore up her gaping holes through which she sucked up a flooding sea. In the morning some of our ships came alongside, and by noon the exhausted *Duncan* had to give up the fight. All except sixty members of her crew, who had been killed in action, were taken off before she went under.

After the battle Admiral Scott moved northward, scouring the sea for scattered transports. The *Salt Lake City* mopped up several wrecked enemy vessels and saw the last Jap heavy cruiser blow up and sink. The admiral, with his surviving ships, returned two hours or so later, satisfied that no more targets were in the vicinity. But an unidentified ship was spotted closing in and the American force prepared to fight.

At that moment a light flashed out a message—the identification signal of the *Boise*. Believing the *Boise* lost, additional identification was asked. It was the *Boise*, all right. Her crew had quelled the fires, stopped up the holes and kept her afloat. The tons of water which had filled her entrails had also helped to douse the blaze. She had a list to starboard but came up to twenty knots with some of her turrets still in serviceable condition.

Captain Mike Moran and his crew had their greatest wish fulfilled at last. For weeks they had cruised with task forces hither and yon, but always seemed to miss the fight. The *Boise*, which had come to be nicknamed "The Reluctant Dragon," during these past hours had wiped that name off the books and her rightful one had been restored. She was again the *Boise*, the "one-ship fleet."

During the hottest minutes of the fight, when the *Boise* was in the center of the American formation and all the Japs appeared to be firing at her simultaneously, Moran is reported to have remarked, to no one in particular: "Why do the Japs persist in making these center plays?" The remainder of his less printable remarks was lost in the sound of gunfire and exploding shells.

Only two enemy destroyers survived this toe-to-toe, gun-to-gun slugging match. For the loss of the *Duncan*, and two cruisers and another destroyer damaged, our forces had destroyed three heavy cruisers, one 6-inch-gun cruiser and four destroyers. Reports say that at least one other enemy auxiliary or destroyer was sunk.

It was evident that the Japanese were stirred up, judging by their renewed air and sea assaults on Henderson Field. Twice on the afternoon of the thirteenth they bombed the airfield. After dark they followed up with a surface force including at least one battleship. The next day two more waves of enemy bombers came over. The first formation, about twenty-five twin-engined planes escorted by fighters, dropped their missiles before they could be intercepted. The second formation was caught, and nine of the fifteen bombers and eleven of the escorting Zeros were destroyed. We lost only one fighter.

The enemy was persistent. Again, early on October 15, a convoy of transports, protected by a battleship, cruisers and destroyers, was sighted off Savo. Other heavy Jap units were observed around the Guadalcanal area. The Japanese prepared to get these fresh troops and supplies ashore, west of our positions.

Undeterred by this display of power, our tiny air force, only a short flight away on Guadalcanal, stabbed at the invaders with bombs and machine guns. The result was three direct heavy bomb hits on one transport and two hits on two others. The battleship, too, suffered from bomb hits and one Jap fighter plane was shot down.

Our forces on Guadalcanal were fighting as strongly as their weapons permitted. The arrival of the *Hornet* in early October had brought some much-needed relief, causing the Japs at least a little discomfort.

Of an attack at this time on Buin-Faisi, about three hundred miles northwest of Guadalcanal, one of the *Hornet's* airmen reported: "We got up early to catch the Japs asleep. The weather was bad when we arrived and we got separated because of the poor visibility. We bombed our objectives by climbing on instruments, making a procedure turn and coming down. If you had a ship in your sights when your plane broke through the overcast into the clear, you bombed it. If you didn't have one, then you were too low to correct your dive and had to climb and try again. We know that we damaged a transport and an aviation tender. The overcast prevented us from seeing any further results of the attack."

Some time thereafter the *Hornet* retired briefly, but some of her planes stayed on Henderson Field to keep punching at the Japs. They directed one of their blows at Rekata Bay on October 16, in an effort to slow down Jap strength pouring into Guadalcanal and to nip off some of the nuisance bombardments which had turned many a night into living hell for our troops.

One flier relates: "We got twelve Zeros, a big float plane, a gasoline and ammunition dump, supplies and anti-aircraft batteries. Our punch wasn't very heavy, though. Our Guadalcanal airfield had been shot to bits by enemy warships and the garrison had only five machines still able to fly. From Henderson we struck at beached Jap transports and got some. Then, on October 20, the *Hornet* returned and we went aboard her."

During this period our forces had succeeded in running small numbers of reinforcements ashore on Guadalcanal, along with some supplies loaded on old four-stacker destroyers of World War I vintage. This same type of ship brought in gasoline and bombs. Each stripped, converted destroyer was able to carry about a hundred and fifty men and their equipment. They were paving the way for larger convoys, and meanwhile, with their help, our forces would hold out as long as this ferry service continued to operate.

Chapter 8

"TEMPERED"

THE *Enterprise* and *Hornet* had scarcely joined forces on October 24 when our long-range reconnaissance planes reported a large enemy fleet composed of several carriers, battleships, numerous cruisers, destroyers and some transports. It was preparing to steam southward, obviously to meet up with the many scattered warship flotillas then operating in the southern Solomons. Should this fleet succeed in joining with the large number of Japanese warships already operating in the Guadalcanal area, it would give the enemy the most puissant concentration of naval power yet assembled.

Our two-carrier force, including a new 35,000-ton battleship, set a north-northwest course which led directly to Guadalcanal. Still too far removed for air contact, the enemy's movements were followed closely by our Navy airmen who operated Catalinas out of Guadalcanal. Slow and incapable of fast, evasive action, they presented easy targets and were undeceived about it. With superb, quiet heroism, one of the Catalina crews added to its report that day: "We are being attacked by Zeros. Please notify our next of kin."

The American carrier force steamed on through the afternoon. The Reapers, tense in their ready room, reviewed once more all the combat tactics practiced so thoroughly during the three and a half months. Leppla, Vejtasa, Faulkner and Flatley, the veterans, were under a constant barrage of questions, mostly about the Jap pilots and planes. Strong hands were executing intricate air maneuvers, demonstrating dives, shooting runs and skillful parries to the less experienced,

120

rehearsing the thousand and one little tricks which help preserve a pilot's life.

Making a last checkup on deck, Flatley moved over to the Wildcats, felt a wing here and a prop there, asked an occasional question of the laboring ground crew and threw examining glances at engines and guns, air frames and instruments. Earlier he had watched the replacements of broken parts, the mending of bullet holes, the fitting of new mechanisms into the guns, the tuning up of engines, and the testing of instruments and electrical equipment. He had assured himself that everything was in order, that his planes were ready to be taken up in as perfect condition as it was humanly possible to make them.

"After dinner that night," Flatley related many months later, "my mind was filled with thoughts of the Reapers and their coming test. I had no worries about their ability to take care of themselves. They had worked hard and long, and they were well prepared and ready for combat.

"How well they were prepared spiritually, however, gave me some concern. Many of them were very young and many not too religious. Those who were, of course, could always seek out the ship's chaplain. Those who weren't were more or less my responsibility, I felt. We had done a good job of preparing them to fight. Now it was somebody's job to prepare them to die, if that was to be their fate.

"It wasn't my intention to call them together and preach a sermon. I sat down, instead, and wrote out a letter to all of them. They could read it in the privacy of their cabins. It ran something like this: 'Doubtless you have been raised a Christian, even though you may profess no specific belief. All Christianity vocally or audibly or tacitly acknowledges that there is a Supreme Being, usually referred to as God. The Bible tells us that God is our Maker. That He created us. That He gave us a free will and a conscience. He also gave us Ten Commandments to guide us in our daily relations with our fellow men. He told us that if we obeyed these commandments to the best of our ability we could be rewarded after death by being received into Heaven, and conversely, if we deliberately disobeyed them, we would be justly punished.

" 'Now God, in His wisdom, knows the weakness and frailty of the human being. He knows of the many temptations and pitfalls that beset us. He only asks us to do our level best to keep His commandments. However, we are not perfect and every man is guilty of failure in great or less degree.

" 'Therefore, in His justice, God is willing to forgive, if the transgressor, having failed, is truly sorry for his sin and firmly resolves that he will do his best not to commit the sin again.

" 'What is all this leading up to? Only this. We are fighting a war today against enemies who for the most part are not Christian, who deny the existence of God—the Nazis and the Japs.

" 'We are not a warlike people. We love peace and the fruit of peace; we fight heathen enemies who not only seek economic gain but who would stamp out Christianity if they are victorious. We have every reason to expect our God to be on our side. Ever since His birth, two thousand years ago, one ruler or another has attempted to eliminate Christianity from the earth. So far no one has been successful.

" 'If we believe in God, and we do; if we believe in His infallible wisdom and justice, which we should, then we can rightly ask ourselves: If we are Christians and beloved by God, why are we being subjected to this worldwide conflict?

" 'The only logical answer, both from a historical and theological analysis, is that, as Christians, we have failed. We have allowed ourselves to become soft. We have disregarded God and His commandments. Our wills have become weak. Our consciences hardened. We have offended God and as

Christian nations are little better than the heathens. In other words, we have become hypocrites, professing one thing outwardly and practicing another.

" 'What's the answer? The answer is a return to God. How can we return? By getting down on our knees and praying, or just praying if we don't believe in kneeling. By professing anew, or maybe for the first time, our belief in God. By asking for His aid. By telling Him we are sorry for past transgressions. By promising Him that we will lead a better life in the future. By professing a love for Him who made us. By asking for His blessings and particularly for the strength to do our duty bravely. And that duty today is to meet our enemies, who are God's enemies, courageously and without fear, secure in the knowledge that what we are fighting for is right.'

"When we were gathered for a last talk before turning in that night, although none of the Reapers spoke of it, I felt that they had all understood. My mind was much more at rest."

The morning broke bright and clear as the American task force neared the Santa Cruz Island arc. Long before it was light the two carriers turned into the breeze, ready to launch scouts and combat patrols.

The Catalinas had continued their watch through the night and the enemy had maintained his heading for the past twenty-four hours. By sunset the two opposing forces should be within about two hundred miles of each other.

On the carriers the pilots were in their cockpits, engines idling, and the plane-handling crews stood by the wheel chocks. The launching officer waved for the leading plane to taxi to the starting line. There the pilot would put on the brakes and rev up the engine, waiting for the launching officer to take a quick look to the bow for safety's sake, and then give the take-off signal. The Reapers took to the air in sections and flew their combat patrols, Flatley arranging for the every man to get at least four hours flying that day.

The presence of the new battleship had revived much speculation among the ships' crews. From the deck of the carrier everyone had seen the man-o'-war thrust her great bulk through the light swells, and had the opportunity to evaluate her numerous weapons, from the 5-inchers and 40-mm. Bofor automatics, mounted to be fired almost vertically as well as horizontally, up to the new high-power 20-mm. Oerlikons, and .50-caliber machine guns. There were also nine big 16-inch rifles, housed in three turrets, which fire projectiles of 2000 pounds and are reserved mainly for enemy warships or shore installations.

The ship itself was the latest word in super dreadnaughts. Unlike the earlier types, some of which we lost at Pearl Harbor, this vessel had been laid down to fight both surface ships and aircraft. Its floating gun platform, some 700 feet from bow to stern, measured 108 feet at its widest part. Its low sides were covered with thick, tough armor plate from just below the water line, shielding the ship's vital insides against horizontally fired shells. Her torpedo blanket and her internal compartmentation for localizing the water inrush if punctured by torpedoes set her apart from older battle wagons.

Heavy projectiles, fired at ranges greater than eight or ten miles, fall steeply at the end of their trajectory; therefore the modern battleship is also protected by one or two armored decks to withstand plunging fire and falling bombs, as is the tower forward of the funnel which harbors the controls. Heavily armored gun turrets shelter the gunners and keep out fragments of bursting shells, bombs and the machine-gun bullets of strafing planes.

Having a long range, the anti-aircraft batteries are able to fire their high explosive shells up to more than 30,000 feet, since their missiles are equipped with a fuse which can be set to explode at the desired distance.

Everyone in the task force was eager to see this mighty ship go into action.

The American force now split into two units and steamed approximately ten miles apart. The *Hornet* was escorted by cruisers and some destroyers, and the *Enterprise* by the new battleship, destroyers and some cruisers.

The elementary principle in sea-air naval war is to deliver the main attack against carriers; therefore Captain Thomas L. Gatch, of Annapolis, Maryland, commander of the battleship, formed detailed plans to hug the carrier and use his craft's enormous fire power to cover the *Enterprise* with an umbrella of steel. The cruisers and destroyers were disposed near the carrier and battleship.

About 2:30 P.M. a Catalina spotted and radioed the Jap position. Before dusk the opposing forces would be within about two hundred miles of each other. An admiral's staff conference was called, and half an hour later Air Group Commander Richard Gaines gave word to launch attack squadrons within thirty minutes to contact, assault and return before dark. The gongs clanged and the Reapers, detailed to escort the attack group on the long mission, climbed into their machines. The Reapers gave the slower Dauntlesses and Avengers a head start, because of the extreme distance. To accompany them at their slow cruising speed would mean a weaving back and forth for the fighters and thus a waste of gas. They would overtake them before the attackers reached their objective.

"As planned," Commander Flatley recalls, "we picked up our attack group. In the distance were the *Hornet's* squadrons, all formed and flying toward a pin point on their charts where they hoped to locate the Japs. We reached the area, and although it was a clear day and we had the wide visibility of the late afternoon sun in our favor, below us lay nothing but a vast expanse of ocean. From 15,000 feet, the air group commander had a view of the sea for forty miles all around. There was no enemy fleet.

"We went on for thirty minutes more, and when there was still no sign we got orders to turn back. Reluctantly we changed direction and plotted our return course. In our anxiety to engage the enemy, we'd stretched our flight to just a trifle over the safety margin. It would take all our skill and ingenuity to coax engines and planes and our dwindling gasoline supply into getting us home without a ducking.

"Darkness had closed in when we finally arrived over the carrier and we were faced with wartime night landings, the very thing we had hoped to avoid. It is no trouble to experienced pilots, who have had thorough practice in night flying, but I was a bit worried about my younger Reapers. However, I needn't have been. When it was their turn, they came wheeling into the landing circle, carefully watched the signal officer's light directions, which take the place of the flags used in daylight, and landed like veterans. I was proud of the way they handled this emergency.

"We had one mishap. Lieutenant Frank Miller, out of fuel, had been forced to land about seventy miles from the carrier. A destroyer was dispatched immediately, but in spite of a careful search we couldn't locate him. It was our first loss."

Earlier in the afternoon there had been one other incident. Lieutenant (Bill) Blair was flying combat patrol when his automatic propeller went haywire and stuck in full pitch. Bill signaled that he would have to go into the water unless the commander would risk having him shoot a landing aboard. (In a Wildcat, when the prop is stuck in high pitch, the pilot cannot make the usual landing. He loses proper control and can't throttle back, because the propeller pitch can't be changed to take the finer bite of air necessary, which ordinarily enables him to maintain control at low speed. The alternative is for the pilot to make a glide approach from directly astern and lower his flaps cautiously to slow the machine down as much as possible.)

It was decided to let Blair risk it. He waited until they were ready for him, then flew off astern for altitude, nosed down and aimed for the deck. The carrier, of course, was running away at top speed. Bill did everything beautifully, and the instant he set her down, everyone was about to breathe again. But the Wildcat bounced, the hook missed the arresting gear and his machine leaped over the fence, crashing into two Dauntless scout bombers. There was the harsh screech of crushing duralumin.

When the three planes were separated, only the tail sections of the two scouts had been wrecked, but the Wildcat was in a sad state. Blair stepped out unharmed.

Confronted with the possibility of battle at any moment, there was no time to move other planes on deck and get the damaged machines below for repair. The mechanics had to shove them overside to keep the flight deck clear for operations. It was a blow to lose three machines just before an action, but it couldn't be helped. Mechanical failures will happen from time to time and mechanical props are still delicate things which sometimes pack up for no apparent reason.

There was another conference that night and plans were made for the following day. Battle was imminent. It was only a matter of who would get in the first punch. The staff stayed up all night to scan the latest reports as they came in —as did the aircraftsmen, who were working under canvas shades on the flight deck and below on the hangar deck. They toiled all night to guarantee that every plane would be in the best possible condition.

There was a turnout when the gongs clanged before dawn. With the certain knowledge that it was well within range of the enemy, our fleet could not afford to leave any margin for error. It was important that we get our air attack group off to strike before the enemy's aircraft hit at our carriers. The Catalinas, presumably dogging the Jap warships, had not reported for several hours. We had to dispatch our own scouts to locate the enemy position definitely before sending in our aircraft.

Shortly before dawn twenty SBDs roared aloft and fanned out in pairs on their separate courses. Lieutenant Commander "Bucky" Lee, skipper of the *Enterprise's* Scouting 10, had estimated the enemy's approximate position and then marked out segments radiating roughly over one third of the circle to the northwest-northeast. He sent his scouts off in nine pairs, while he and his wing man took the line that led directly to the position he figured the enemy would be.

Lee's reckoning had been correct. At 8:10 A.M. he reported position, speed, course and disposition of the Jap fleet. He and his wing man were subjected to heavy attacks by defending Zeros but fought their way through, bringing two planes down in flames.

Far out on the furthest scouting leg to the west, Lieutenant Stockton Birney Strong and Ensign C. V. ("Chuck") Irvine had flown their search and were about to return when they heard their skipper's contact report. Strong made some hasty computations. He had flown more than two hundred miles; the reported position of the enemy was more than a hundred miles off and from there it would be roughly another two hundred miles to his carrier. If he used his gas supply sparingly and did not have to fight very much, he could swing over and bomb the Jap force.

He advised his wing mate of this intention. Irvine radioed back: "Lead on, Lieutenant, I'll follow."

The two slow scouts winged their way across the sky. Sighting the enemy, they picked out a large carrier, dived through the screen of Zeros and the ack-ack thrown up by the escort vessels, and swooped low in a 75-degree dive, their eyes fastened to their telescopic sights, until they were at 1000 feet. They pulled their Mickey Mouse and leveled off. The bombs smashed through the carrier's deck, blossoming out into flame. Then the two pilots raced for home, hugging the water closely to escape pursuing Zeros.

Lieutenant Strong, a veteran of the Coral Sea, had no orders to attack, and realized how small were his chances of getting away unscathed before he left his search area. Nonetheless, he engineered and carried out a project far above his line of duty. The deed earned him a recommendation for the Congressional Medal of Honor. Later he was given the Navy Cross. Commander Flatley asked Strong what motivated him to face such danger, voluntarily and unprotected. The young lieutenant told him: "I couldn't forget the sight of my carrier after it was bombed in the Solomons last August. The bodies of my shipmates, all twisted and charred, were spread around where the bomb had exploded. Right then I made up my mind to prevent the enemy from dropping a bomb on my ship again, at any cost."

Bucky Lee's contact report had set the attack machinery in motion. The *Hornet's* dive bombers and torpedo planes went off in three waves, each escorted by fighters. First came the TBD's (Dauntless dive bombers), under their skipper, Gus Widhelm, with a Wildcat escort commanded by Lieutenant Commander Mike Sanchez. Then followed Scouting Squadron Eight and finally, a torpedo-plane squadron.

While these planes were being launched from the *Hornet,* the *Enterprise* sent her striking force into the air. Flatley, still suffering from his injured foot, led a four-plane section of Reapers who were to accompany the attack group. With him went Ensigns Russ Reiserer, R. R. Witte and E. B. Coalson. Lieutenant Leppla led the second four-plane escort section. With him were Ensigns R. E. ("Dusty") Rhodes, A. E. Mead and W. B. ("Chip") Reding.

The slower Dauntless machines set the pace, due to the

different speeds of the three types of aircraft. Astern came the Avengers, with Flatley's four Wildcats cruising to starboard and Leppla's stationed in a similar position to port. The planes climbed steadily into a darkening, low-ceiling sky. Clouds and mist had begun to thicken.

Abruptly, like a lightning flash, a squadron of Jap fighters struck at the formation, scoring two hits. They had not been spotted until they were within a couple of seconds' flight from the leading Dauntless bombers. It was then only about 9 A.M. and the group had flown not more than sixty of the two hundred miles which separated the American carriers from the enemy.

At the moment of the attack Flatley's section was turned away slightly. Leppla made a valiant effort to dive and interpose his planes, but the Japs struck too swiftly.

Before the Zeros could reform for the next attack, Leppla intercepted and fought so fiercely that he succeeded, with his men, in pulling the Japs off the bombers, who continued ahead at their measured speed. Flatley, meanwhile, had turned and was closing in when he saw a single Zero ahead of and below his charges, on the verge of zooming up to deliver an underside attack. Jimmy waggled his wings, signaling to the remainder of his flight, and dived to cut him off. In unison, the Reapers jumped the Jap and downed him.

During these few minutes the formation had covered about five miles. Leppla, Rhodes, Mead and Coalson were far astern, battling for their lives. Jimmy's first impulse was to take his section back to help out, but since his prime mission was to protect the bombers, he reorganized his Reapers and returned to a position above his charges.

Piecing together information gathered from others who witnessed the action from a distance, Jim learned later that Leppla and his three comrades fought a dozen Japs before they were overwhelmed. Having been foiled in their first attack on the bombers, the Japs began darting in from above on the port side, forcing the Reapers to turn outward to get their noses up at the attackers. They appeared to concentrate on Leppla, although there were always at least two Zeros attacking each of the other Reapers.

One pair of Japs poured a long thrust into Leppla's Wildcat, after he shot down one Zero which had damaged his engine. Mead, flying with him, shot up another. Rhodes followed suit, and Chip Reding, the only survivor, got a side shot at one. Reding, who saw smoke trailing from Rhodes's plane as they flew their defensive pattern to hold off the enemy, noticed that Rhodes had not fired for some time. It was obvious his guns no longer functioned. Chip watched his haul the nose of his plane up to kill speed, open his coop and dive overboard. When last seen, Dusty's chute had opened. He was carried away by the wind.

Chip, left alone with a swarm of number-one Jap fighters, was in no condition to fight. His Wildcat was badly shot up. A 20-mm. shell had exploded inside the dashboard and wrecked all his electrical equipment. It had cut out his guns, radio and automatic prop control. Another shell had burst in the stabilizer. The wings and fuselage were riddled with machine-gun bullets. He put his Wildcat into a steep dive. Two Zeros stayed with him until he pulled out just above the sea; then he lost them. Inasmuch as our carriers, too, were under attack, Chip had to skip around in the air for three hours before he could take his battered plane home at last. Leppla, Rhodes and Mead were reported to have bailed out in their parachutes. That was the last seen of them.

Meanwhile, the hostile fleet had split into several groups. Battleships, cruisers and the main force of destroyers steamed in single column about sixty miles ahead of their carriers. Aside from the flat-top set afire by Strong and Irvine some hours earlier, and now trailing the others, there were probably two more carriers in the force.

By 11 A.M., Flatley was losing sight of the *Hornet's* two attack groups. The dive bombers had made a slight course change and disappeared to port. A second *Hornet* formation was astern. About fifteen minutes later he discovered a column of Jap warships, including two battleships and a strong force of cruisers and destroyers, but there were no carriers visible.

Of the continuing search, Flatley reports: "Russ, Witte, Coalson and I were protecting three dive bombers led by Ensign Estes, and four torpedo planes led by Lieutenant McDonald Thompson. The remainder of our force had become separated as we flew through the cloud bank and had tagged on behind Gus Widhelm's formation. We saw no carriers and wanted to continue our search for them. However, we'd already flown about as far as we could, and since we had dropped our wing tanks when we were attacked earlier, we decided to settle for the fleet beneath us, instead.

"Two heavy cruisers were the targets. Estes selected one for his dive bombers and Thompson the second for his torpedo planes. There were no Zeros around. I wondered about that, and later we learned that they had attacked Widhelm's formation and carried on a long, running fight, leaving their ships exposed."

The four torpedo planes circled to a lower altitude and stationed themselves on either beam. To draw off some of the ack-ack fire, the Reapers determined to dive and strafe. While Thompson took his TBFs down to attack position, the Reapers descended to 11,000 feet, then dropped to 8000, into cumulus clouds.

"From there," Flatley's report continues, "we watched the four torpedo planes swing wide and lose altitude until they were at about 5000 feet, and about two miles from the cruiser. Then they swung in and started a fast, slanting attack with their noses down, yawing from side to side to upset the aim of the ship gunners. At the same time we turned over for the dive. We had split up to strike from different directions. We came down at about sixty degrees and we could see the Japs first firing their heavy guns at the torpedo planes, and then opening fire with their light automatics.

"As soon as they saw us they swung half their armament upward to ward us off. The TBFs dropped their 'fish,' banked sharply and turned away, zigzagging violently.

"We began to fire our .50s at 3500 feet, just a short burst to upset the Jap gunners, then held our fire for the next thousand feet until we began to open up with all guns. There was a scattering of sparks as our tracers bit into steel and wood.

"All the planes pulled away and re-formed to return to base. Estes' group had sent two of their 1000-pounders smashing into a cruiser. It was burning hotly and seemed to be in considerable trouble. The second *Hornet* attack formation was getting results too. As we retired, we could see its bombs and torpedoes send up great spouts of flame and water."

Gus Widhelm led his squadron of bombers north and sighted a Jap battleship, cruisers and destroyers. When one of his pilots queried over the intercom if they were going to attack this column, Gus's radio chuckled back: "They're only chicken feed. We're looking for carriers."

About fifteen miles past the battleship the squadron was attacked by a horde of Zeros. The leading Zero flew straight at Gus in a head-on attack. Gus countered with his bow guns. The Jap burst into flame about a hundred yards in front and tried to ram Gus, but Widhelm dived under him. The Jap fell astern. The second Zero came up from underneath. Gus kept a half cowling on him and fired ahead, then held the firing button down until the Jap flew into his bullets and exploded. As usual, the Jap fighters selected the squadron leader and concentrated on him. (Our fighters do the same, having discovered that when they get the leader the Jap formation usually breaks up, making it easier to kill off the others.)

George Stokely acted as Gus's fire-control director. With an eye on the enemy, he kept Gus informed of the directions from which the Japs were coming, allowing the leader to turn his whole squadron and set up the rear free gunners every chance he had to do so.

Whenever there was occasion for Gus to talk over his radio with Mike Sanchez, the skipper of the escorting fighters, the communication would open with such identification as: "Gus to Mike," or "Mike to Gus." Suddenly a husky voice, fairly oozing a Japanese accent, broke into their earphones: "Mike from Gus . . . return to base all planes." Later, they laughed over the Jap's attempt to disrupt formation and morale.

Gus believes that they faced the Japs' number one team, but according to him, it wasn't so much. At one stage of the battle Stokely yelled: "Mr. Widhelm, look!" Gus looked and saw a Zero with both wings shot off. There the Jap sat, forsaken in his fuselage, before it dropped like a plummet.

While Gus's outfit was knocking down a dozen planes one of the Nips nipped him. Widhelm says: "The guy sat up above me. He'd start down and I'd feint him. He was an old-timer and stayed right up there. He made three passes. On the fourth pass, when another Jap was coming in from the right, he came down and deliberately took a full deflection shot. He hit the oil lines, somewhere in the cooler (the oil radiator). I knew I was hit when I heard the bullets drill into the metal. Then the oil sprayed into the cockpit. It gushed all over me."

But Gus kept going. There was nowhere to turn for safety; besides, he didn't want to have someone else take the attack aimed at him, the leader. The running fight had carried him well out of range of Jap flak. His engine continued to run for ten more minutes before it froze up and he had to drop out of formation. A Zero followed close on his tail. Gus cork-screwed, and in an almost vertical 300-mile-per-hour dive, he lost the Zero. In spite of the big holes blasted in its wings by 20-mm. cannon shells, and a chewed-off tail assembly, the Dauntless stood the strain of the twisting dive. Gus jetti-soned his 1000-pound bomb to lighten the machine and tried to get as far as possible from the Jap carriers. "My boys didn't lose formation when I fell out; they kept their tactics and they kept their heads, and that was the only thing that saved the attack," Gus explained.

While he skidded down, the squadron attacked a giant carrier of the *Zuikaku* class. Seven planes scored hits with their 1000-pounders, setting the vessel afire from end to end.

Widhelm hit the water hard. As the plane brought up to a neck-breaking stop, its nose went under. The engine was so hot that the water around it boiled. The sudden arresting of the plane sheared the pin that holds the cockpit hood open and locked him inside.

The cockpit filled with water in the few seconds it took him to force the cover open. He yelled for Stokeley to get his parachute. The rubber boat needed no special attention. It had been so fixed that if Stokely held the wooden toggle he would wind up with the inflated raft. Gus had his own parachute, maps, navigation chart board, quinine and him-self out of the plane within fifteen seconds. They were also equipped with pistols and knives. Both swam away from the oil slick before climbing into the boat. Widhelm penciled their position on the side of the rubber raft and Stokely be-gan to clean the guns.

A little later they saw two *Kongo* class battleships coming over the horizon to the south. They stowed their pistol parts into the raft's zipper pocket, tied everything else to the boat, turned it over and hid underneath. The warships came within four miles of them and steamed past. Peering out from under the raft, they saw enemy aircraft, out of fuel, land in the water near by. Jap destroyers picked up the pilots.

There were sharks around the boat, which the two fliers frightened away by violent splashing. They righted the boat and climbed back when the battleships and destroyers went out of sight.

Not long after, a second formation of Jap vessels approached. Again they overturned the boat and hid underneath. When they came up for a look, they thought the end had come for certain. A Jap destroyer, about a hundred yards away, was headed directly for them. Reasoning that it was useless to hide, they climbed back into the boat.

The destroyer, slowing down, was now almost on top of them. Officers on the deck and bridge were eying them through binoculars. A sailor at the rail, with a line in his hand, was waiting for the order to throw it.

Widhelm and Stokely decided hastily to make a great show of trying to catch the line if it were thrown, but to miss it accidentally. They felt the Japs might shoot if they refused to catch it at all. But the destroyer slid past. Her bow wave washed the raft away from the ship; the sailor never moved.

The destroyer flashed a signal to a ship closing in behind it. The young Americans frantically hid everything they had. Rank badges went overboard and Widhelm held his chart board overside to let it go instantly, if necessary.

The first destroyer had passed about ten feet away. "No signals were exchanged and no shots fired by either side," Widhelm says. The second ship, a cruiser, passed also, turned and swept by at only thirty feet. They saw that she had been hit by a bomb. The explosion had wrecked a plane sitting on the catapult and damaged the superstructure. There had been a hot fire. They noticed that the metal had melted and run with the heat, but the cruiser appeared to be able to steam and steer well enough.

This cruiser signaled to a destroyer astern, and the vessel

veered and headed directly for them. It appeared intent on running them down. The fliers wanted to give the impression that they had nothing except the bare rubber boat, and above all didn't want it known that they had oars, so they paddled with their hands to get out of the ship's path.

"It steamed past, too," Widhelm recounts. "The enlisted crew waved and we waved back. They all had a nice set of teeth, we noticed when they grinned at us."

Evidently satisfied that the fliers would die on the raft or, at best, get washed up on one of their islands, the Japs steamed away. Widhelm and Stokely got out their oars and paddled rapidly away from this too busy Jap thoroughfare.

They had emergency rations for thirty days and two canteens of fresh water, and so rationed themselves to a canteen cup full of water each sundown so that their bodies would have all night to soak up the liquid. With it, they consumed half a can of rations. It came in small caviar tins and, as Widhelm recollects: "It looked like fruit cake and tasted like fruit cake, and probably was fruit cake."

The two were trying to navigate to the south by using one pilot 'chute as a sea anchor when the wind was unfavorable, but they weren't getting far. So they made three sails from a parachute. Ballooned out in the daytime, they dried and were ready to double as coverings at night, when lapping waves and spray soaked them through and through.

When Stokely asked where they might end up if they just drifted and didn't attempt to sail, Widhelm suggested that probably it would be Jap-held Truk.

"Boy, won't they be surprised when we try to take that base!" Stokely commented. Another time, they thought they heard a submarine running under water. They formed plans immediately as to what they would do if it surfaced, and agreed on shooting the first man who showed his face on deck. Stokely even thought they were "likely to take that thing over," if it surfaced.

On the third day, both were asleep when an American patrol plane spotted them. They woke up only when its engines roared overhead. The pilot dropped a float light to see the wind direction. It failed to burn, so the resourceful Widhelm made a wind sock out of a piece of parachute. As the plane hit hard on the waves, Stokely advanced the idea of drinking the rest of the water in their canteens. Both took healthy pulls, certain now of being saved. O'Dowd, the rescue boat's pilot, turned out to be a former pupil of Widhelm's whom he had put through flight training when he was an instructor at Pensacola. It was a fitting conclusion to their adventure.

Luck appeared to be wholly on Widhelm's side. On the night he was taken back to an advanced island base he joined some Army fliers in a small crap game. As he pocketed his winnings, $1250 in all, one Army man murmured: "We should have known you can't beat him. First Midway, then Santa Cruz, three days in a rubber boat—and now this!"

After a few days of rest Gus returned to his squadron, proceeded to Guadalcanal when the big show was on through November 14–16, and witnessed the *San Francisco's* great battle.

"Widhelm is ready again" was his favorite expression. The Japs had better be!

While these engagements went on, and the American forces were inflicting damage on three Jap carriers, a battleship and five cruisers, the Japs were by no means idle. As our dive bombers, torpedo planes and fighters hammered at the Japanese fleet two hundred miles to the north, the enemy's air striking force hurled a prolonged assault against our warships. Following the pattern of May 8 in the Coral Sea, both fleets had located each other and pulled no punches.

After launching their planes about 9 A.M., the two American carriers had slipped back inside their screen of ships and spread about ten miles apart. The battleships had been brought in near the *Enterprise,* from which point Captain Gatch followed carefully the carrier's violent, twisting course changes during battle as she swung sharply from side to side to upset the enemy's aim. The cruisers had edged in to 1500 yards, a distance necessary to avert collision, and the destroyers were wreathing gracefully along the periphery, their sensitive asdics tuned to submarine Diesels.

The Reaper section, which had been held back for defense, was divided into two groups. One group was in the air on combat patrol, and the same number waited on deck to relieve them should there by no attack within an hour. That would allow the first group to refuel and be ready for a prompt take-off in case hostile planes drew near. It was most important that they have a maximum gas load in their tanks at all times.

Ensigns Jim Billo, J. E. Caldwell and Bobby Edwards had been out and up at 20,000 feet when Leppla's section was being attacked. Edwards' prop, which was not functioning well, forced him down to seek a landing. Billo and Cadwell, however, swung around to Leppla's aid. As they neared, they saw eight Zeros pouncing on a single Wildcat. They thought it might be Leppla. The Wildcat set one opponent afire and then drew around to down a second. Having picked their victims, Billo and Caldwell dived. Billo got his Jap with one long burst and pulled out for a second attack when tracers passed his machine. A Zero sat on his tail, sawing back and forth in an effort to correct his aim. Billo put his nose down to shake off the Jap. He got rid of the pest, flattened out, and climbed back upstairs.

A 'chute floated seaward a little distance away. There was no sign of Caldwell, nor of what he had taken to be Leppla. It might have been either one of the two. He cruised around, looking for someone to join up with, and finding three Wildcats from VF-8 (off the *Hornet*), he grouped with them.

Word of the approach of Jap dive bombers had found Swede Vejtasa, and other Reapers aboard the *Enterprise*, ready to take to the air. Swede led his flight toward the *Hornet* and had clawed up to 12,000 feet when he saw the bombers. Twenty-four Aichis had split into two groups. One section was already attacking the *Hornet*. He could see the black puffs of shell bursts over the carrier. The second group was slanting in a full power glide toward the turnover point. They were above his section and moving fast.

The leading Aichis pushed through a cloud layer and emerged at Swede's level in his bombing dive. A steep wing-over and a high-side attack run on Swede's part brought the Jap down. The others passed about 2000 feet overhead, executed their turnover and began their dive for the carrier. Swede's group followed them into the anti-aircraft curtain and through the screen of machine-gun fire, but they were too far ahead to be caught in the dive. The Reaper section did not get within shooting range until the Japs had dropped their bombs and flattened out to escape. Although their rear gunners opened fire at the pursuing planes, the enemy pilots made no defensive maneuvers and continued on their course. Two of them, attacked from above, tumbled into the sea.

The American airmen began climbing to look for other enemy planes. Swede's engine cut out as he was drawing fuel from his wing tanks. He switched back over to the main tank and the engine caught. Only then he noticed a fine gasoline spray from the punctured side tank, evidently shot through by Jap bullets. He released the tank and let it drop.

Back at 10,000 feet, the flight was told to watch out for Mitsu 97s, torpedo planes. A group of Aichis was already being attack by two Reapers, who brought them down just outside the umbrella of bursting 5-inch shells thrown up by the ships.

Several other ships fell victim to the Reapers' machine

guns and the anti-aircraft fire. The 5-inch shells were bursting in such close groups, and their pattern was so dense, that several Jap pilots pulled out of their dives at 7000 feet and turned tail.

At this point the fighter director was instructing Ensign W. H. ("Hank") Leder, who led another Reaper group, to proceed north in search of Mitsus. Since he was above Hank's section, Swede followed the new directive. Ten miles out on this new course, Hank gave the "tallyho!" adding, "Nine o'clock. Down."

Swede, now at 13,000 feet, dropped and spotted the torpedo planes at about 7000 feet. There were eleven of them in a step-up column of three two-plane flights and one three-plane flight. Lieutenant Stan Ruehlow, leader of Swede's second section, and his wing man had dropped down to attack two Zeros only a moment before this, and as Swede dived he could see them already at work on the torpedo planes. The Mitsus' smooth dark paint made them easily distinguishable. Swede's dive built up his speed to about 400 miles per hour, and the Japs, slanting down in full power glide, were clocking about 300.

The Mitsus were flying under a cloud and about to break formation to make their attack run against the carrier from different angles when Harris and Swede lashed into the nearest three-plane section, each setting a Mitsu afire. Other star-painted planes set upon other rising suns with equal vengeance. The disturbed Japs broke formation, hauled back out of their dives, and climbed for safety into the clouds.

Swede followed a three-plane section close to him and exploded the number two plane with two short bursts. This left him a clear run toward the leader. He continued his pursuit to close range before he shot from astern. His .50s chewed up the rudder before the plane caught fire and fell away. The third Mitsubishi attempted to get away by making a shallow turn, but the Wildcat came around more quickly.

Though the range was rather wide, the Jap began to smoke after a fairly long burst from Swede's guns.

These three planes were shot down by stern attacks; the Jap rear gunners never had a chance at all. Looking about for the remainder of the Mitsus, Swede drew a bead on a long shot. He gave the ship a blast as he went past; it was a low sideswipe and Swede thought he had missed badly. The Jap was too far above him when Swede emerged from the cloud for another attack, an attack that was unnecessary, because the Nip turned over quite suddenly and fell off in a dive. He crashed on the forecastle of a destroyer, torpedo and all, with a tremendous explosion.

Having already fired seven times, Swede had almost exhausted his ammunition. He was cruising low when two more Jap torpedo planes hove into view, one with a Reaper on his tail. They were retiring from an attack. Swede couldn't resist ganging up on the free plane, and gave the straggling Jap his last few rounds. His bullets drew smoke from the engine, and another five miles further on, the Jap crashed.

Swede was pretty happy to see Harris, who had become separated from him, fly up with Leder and Ruehlow. Harris had bagged one Mitsu and a probable, Ruehlow one Aichi and a probable Mitsu, Leder one Aichi and a probable, and Swede had five Mitsus, two Aichis and one probable. This four-plane Reaper section had shot down ten Japs and had four probables to their credit—all without loss to themselves.

Out of ammunition now, they wanted to refuel and rearm, but were instructed to stay away from their carrier. Too many Japs were still around. They circled the fringe of their ships' anti-aircraft range, nursing their juice for an hour and a half before getting aboard at about 1:20 P.M. Just before they landed they saw a flier bail out of an American plane at 7000 feet and parachute into the sea about twelve miles northwest of the ships. They never found out the man's identity.

The combined guns of the fleet had been pointing skyward all morning, zealous to extend a hot welcome. A 1500-foot ceiling, however, had curtailed their efforts, because it allowed the gunners scarcely more than the flicker of an eye in which to train their guns on the attacking planes from the time they left the clouds to the moment they were close enough to release their bombs. When the third wave of twenty-four torpedo planes and dive bombers finished delivering its drawn-out attack, the overcast had closed to scarcely a thousand feet.

To the men behind the guns, it was not unlike trying to shoot wild game in dense timber; it was snap shooting of the highest order. Standing alert by their weapons, they would have about three seconds to get an enemy plane, or at least to divert its aim. A plane might be spotted by perhaps one gun crew, which would begin to shoot. Others would pick up the fire before seeing the plane, following the direction of the first tracers. Then the dull blur of the diving plane would come into view, to be met by a veritable shower of torrid steel. The Oerlikons' staccato rat-tat-tat-tat would mix with the sharp banging of the 40s, and all the individual sounds would be drowned out by the rising crescendo of crashing firearms.

The first enemy plane had swooped on the *Hornet* at 10:15 A.M. and only a few minutes later, dive bombers had loosed their missiles above the *Enterprise*. The *Hornet* also had absorbed a torpedo early in the fight, causing her speed to drop off. Wave after enemy wave had struck at her again and again. A burning dive bomber, with a dead pilot at the controls, had smashed into the stern edge of her superstructure, causing several casualties. The bomb ripped off its rack, punched a hole through the base of the funnel and dropped into the great smoke pipes leading from the boilers. Stopped in its fall several decks below, the deadly explosive had been disarmed in the dark by the ordnance chief before it could explode. The wreckage of the plane and its spilled gasoline had set fires on several bridge levels. They were scarcely more than under control when a second enemy machine had approached to attack. It was ripped to shreds by the *Hornet's* concentrated fire and crashed on the flight deck. It skidded across and fell into the opening left by the carrier's forward elevator (which had been lowered to bring up a plane), carrying its fire inside the ship.

The *Enterprise* had evaded bombs and torpedoes well enough, although several heavies fell close. One hit and wrecked a section of the vessel, but the damage did not interfere with the ship's operation. Another drilled through the flight deck, slanted out through the open hull on the hangar deck and exploded harmlessly in the sea.

The Mitsu torpedo planes had made their runs from ahead of the carrier, and in an arc, automatically shortening the distance between speeding projectile and oncoming target. The carrier would swing around in an endeavor to present her stern, or if attacked from the side, swerve and offer the narrow target of her beam, rather than her full length.

One Mitsu pilot had made an especially determined effort to see his torpedo hit home. He began his full power glide from the bottom of a cloud far out to starboard. His speed built up to about 250 miles per hour on this downhill run, and his aim was to fly within a few hundred yards of the carrier's beam to get a short broadside shot at her. The Mitsu was spotted leaving the cloud and the ships threw everything they had at him. He passed over the destroyers, came into the fire of the cruisers' automatic weapons, to be picked up a moment later by the battleship's Bofors, Oerlikons, .50s, and also by the carrier's starboard guns. In spite of this converging fire, the Jap persisted and came on. With the range ever shortening, one could picture the pilot sitting there, hunched over the stick, with only one thought in his mind—to get that carrier.

Flight deck of the carrier *Enterprise*, from which the Reapers took off on many of their exploits. (*Official U.S. Navy Photo*)

The carrier *Hornet* lies dead in the water after Japanese warplanes launched a forenoon attack. A second attack damaged her further and she had to be sunk. The other ship . . . . (*Official U. S. Navy Photo*)

For a few interminable seconds the plane appeared to be charmed. Tracers literally ate up the machine, yet it stayed in the air. Then the weight of small projectiles pouring into the Mitsu began to take effect. The tail crumpled. Small explosives pouring in from the side forced the plane to swerve just as the pilot released his torpedo. For a fraction of a minute the machine actually hung in the air, red-hot missiles splitting it to pieces, and as hunks of it fluttered into the water the torpedo sped past the carrier, losing itself in the sea.

The battleship had come under sudden attack, too, when a bomber dived through the overcast, heading straight for it. Although the ship's guns spouted copiously, the bomber did not deviate from its course. Hot lead kept biting into wings and fuselage until, directly above the battleship's bow, the Jap pilot's plane fell apart, shot to pieces, but not before he had freed his big bomb. The bomb struck the edge of the forward turret and exploded there, sending heavy steel chunks ricocheting off the superstructure.

Captain Gatch had left his armored conning tower to get an unbroken view of the attack on the carrier. He faced the two great turrets on the forward end of his ship. A steel apron protected the lower part of his body against flying splinters and bullets, but he was exposed from head to shoulders, and a piece of shrapnel entered his neck. He dropped to the deck, bleeding profusely. If it had not been for the prompt and skilled attention of Chief Quartermaster Ziegler and Quartermaster Johnson, who pinched the vein with their fingers and staunched the flow of blood until medical aid arrived, he might have died before he could be taken to the hospital.

One of his crewmen was killed and others, standing at their posts in exposed positions, were wounded by pieces of the casing. The gunners inside the turret, just two feet from the actual explosion, were unhurt. The armor had proved its toughness.

If a bomb had to strike, it could not have picked a better spot, because the armored turrets are built to withstand the heaviest shells coming at great velocities. If the bomb had landed flush on deck, it might have drilled through and burst below. An explosion there would have caused many casualties and probably would have started fires difficult to control.

Reapers Dave Pollock, Steve Kona, Lyman Fulton and Gerald Davis had been topside since 8:30 A.M., and were cruising when the air striking force took off. They had sighted three Aichis at 16,000 feet, well above the shell bursts of the 5-inch guns. Dave had reported their position to the fighter director and led his Reapers in to attack. At five hundred yards from the nearest plane, he opened with a ranging burst. Then he waited until he was with three hundred and fifty feet to let the Jap have the works. The first shots silenced the rear gunner. Dave closed in further, firing. A tongue of flame began to waver uncertainly along the bottom of the machine, spread to the sides, gained, and enveloped the fuselage. He was so close now that he avoided crashing into the stricken plane only with difficulty.

Kona took care of the second Aichi and Fulton set fire to the third. Fulton never returned from this action. It has been surmised that he ran out of gas and was forced to land in the sea.

Pollock had probed layers of clouds for almost an hour and a half without spotting another Jap. He responded to directions from the carrier which sent him hither and yon, but air action moves fast, and in cloudy conditions, if a plane is not right on the spot, the enemy will have gone from the indicated position in a few seconds, without leaving a trace.

Dave, running low on fuel, dropped down to fill his tanks.

He arrived as another attack was developing and was ordered to intercept. Returning upstairs, Dave and Ensign Dowden, who had also returned for a refill, spotted a torpedo running wild. Obviously, its gyro-controlled rudder was wrecked and locked on one side. Driven ahead by its motors, it spun round and round in circles, endangering vessels in the vicinity, including a slowed-down destroyer, which was picking up one of our pilots. To warn the ship, Dave went down and began to fire short bursts into the water ahead of the torpedo. He hoped they would look to see what he was shooting at, and get out of the torpedo's way. Instead, two destroyers opened fire on him and the other ships followed suit. Range was only a few hundred yards and Dave, fearing they might shoot him down, radioed to tell them of the danger, and to ask that they cease firing. They continued to shoot. Just then the torpedo righted itself, straightened out and exploded with a great blast against the hull of the *Porter*. The destroyer later had to be abandoned and sunk.

Pollock and another Reaper continued to follow carrier directions fifteen miles to the north. They scanned the horizon for a formation of torpedo planes supported by Zeros. The enemy was at 11,000 feet, above a cloud. Already some of his planes were sloping toward the *Enterprise*.

Dave made a run for the nearest plane. It turned out to be a Zero. Unwilling to use up his small store of ammunition on a mere fighter, he hauled around and headed for the nearest torpedo plane. Two Reapers were already working on the starboard side of the formation, so Dave and his wing man picked on the portside Mitsus. He closed with the Japs at about 4000 feet and, attacking from above, shot into one until it smoked and disappeared in the overcast. He had used the last of his ammunition on this one, so he followed it through the cloud and came out on the other side to see the burning Jap machine hit the water and blow up.

Ensign Donald ("Flash") Gordon and Davis had been on combat patrol when the enemy torpedo planes made their run in below them. Flash had pounced on the one nearest to him. His tracer went too high and the alarmed Jap turned away quickly—right into Davis, who was on the other side. Davis kept his guns on him until a plume of smoke rose from the escaping Mitsu. Then the two young Reapers gave their attention to another torpedo plane about to attack. Flash again had the satisfaction of drawing a white, curly feather from the Mitsu's engine. The Jap's rear gunner had evidently been hit, because he did not fire on Flash's second approach. Flash closed in and this time unleashed a burst that exploded the Mitsu about ten feet above the sea.

Davis, his Wildcat smoking, neared the carrier with Flash, who wanted to rearm. But the Japs launched still another attack. "I climbed to 10,000 feet," Flash remembers, "and sighted two dive bombers. I gave both of them a squirt, but they were going too fast and I lost them without being sure if I had scored a hit.

"I was still inside the heavy anti-aircraft curtain, so I climbed out of it and saw another dive bomber. I lined this one up and fired. As I held my finger on the firing button, my guns quit. I was out of ammunition. My last target was smoking and dropping away. Circling, I saw it explode some 4000 feet below.

"After this attack ended, I went low again, hoping to get landed to rearm, when another wave of Japs came over. I flew away from the carrier and was joined by Chip Reding and two other Reapers. Chip was out of ammunition, too.

"We were circling slowly five miles from the fleet at about 500 feet when two Jap torpedo planes approached. They were skimming the waves at no more than ten feet. One of the Reapers dived and fired. Though I had no ammunition, I dived at the other. The Jap must have seen me coming, because he banked sharply—too sharply. His wing flipped the water, brought the Mitsu over in a cartwheel, and spun him into the drink with a big splash."

The number of planes needing to rearm and refuel grew as the minutes passed. One group came low to land and was fired on by the ship's gunners, who were hot on the trigger and fired at everything with wings. The planes tried to make themselves known as friendly, especially to the big battleship, but without success. Finally a voice broke in on their radio: "Keep away from that big — or he'll shoot you down." They kept away. "Big ——" is the name that has stuck to the battleship ever since. On October 2, 1943, the Navy disclosed its real identity as the *South Dakota*. Its score in the Battle of Santa Cruz was thirty-two Jap planes. A few weeks later, on the night of November 14, she bagged three enemy cruisers off the point of Savo Island, in the Solomons.

Three of the Reapers, forced into the sea when their fuel gave out, were picked up by destroyers, and by 2 P.M., after five hours of hard flying, nearly all were aboard.

Torn by crashing enemy planes and charred by fires, the *Hornet* had been staggering under the impact of the ten-hour attack. The order had to be given to torpedo this proud carrier. Two destroyers sank her with torpedoes and shells. All but 129 of her complement of 2900 men were rescued and most of her planes took roost on the *Enterprise*.

The combined ships' guns had brought down 156 Jap planes during this action. The Reaper score sheet showed twenty-one Jap aircraft shot down, twelve probably destroyed. Seven Reapers were missing: Leppla, Mead, Rhodes, Davis, Fulton, Barnes and Caldwell.

Chapter 9

THE REAPERS AT WORK

The *Enterprise*, slightly damaged, dropped back to one of our Pacific outposts, where she anchored in the harbor. Seabees quickly erased all her battle scars, while her squadrons resumed their practice exercises from ashore.

The reverses suffered at Santa Cruz compelled the Japs to revamp completely their plans for an all-out drive to push the American forces off Guadalcanal and into the sea. Before Tokyo's forces could be reorganized for resumption of the Guadalcanal quest, our Navy prepared for the next thrust, and in spite of the prodigious difficulties which had to be overcome to maintain a sizable fleet 4000 miles from our nearest naval base, all the obstacles were gradually surmounted.

Meanwhile, the American air transport system had begun to function almost perfectly. "Sky trains" of Douglas C-47s, and other air transports loaded with urgently needed materials, were on regular runs to Guadalcanal, bringing in cargoes of vital supplies and munitions, and returning to base with wounded men in need of special medical attention.

When the land fighting on the island stepped up again, the Jap army made desperate attempts to confine our invasion forces within the small area already occupied by the Americans and, with the aid of warships, tried to prevent our troops from testing their strength in small jabs at the interior. Nevertheless, reinforced by fresh troops, the Americans were able to drive a bridgehead across Matanikau River, west of

Henderson Field, and from there began to expand and feel out the tired enemy.

To meet the pressure exerted by our newly reinforced garrison, the enemy speeded up the infiltration of troops through the Solomons. Under cover of night, greater numbers of "Pullmans" (cruisers), and "day coaches" (destroyers), of the Tokyo Express pulled in, usually about midnight, and while the destroyers quickly debarked troops and supplies, the cruisers steamed along the coast, bombarding Henderson Field and our positions, and trying to demolish our aircraft scattered in revetments among the torn coconut palms. Around-the-clock harassment, bombing by day and shelling from the sea at night, which had been Jap practice since August 7 and 8, had put the American forces on a twenty-four-hour alert and under a constant strain. It exhausted not only the original landing party, which had been subjected to it incessantly for three months, but also the newest newcomers.

With the arrival of Colonel Evans F. Carlson's Marine Raiders, a slow transformation took place. Landing secretly behind enemy lines, the Raiders began a thirty-day guerrilla war on the Japanese rear. To the enemy, it must have been a nightmare. The Raiders, in strong force, would swoop unexpectedly out of the quiet, tree-covered hills or steaming jungle, send a withering fire into an isolated group of Japs, annihilating them, then disappear back into the timber before the bewildered Nips had a chance to collect their wits. Runners from Jap headquarters, sent out to discover why one or the other of their detachments had failed to return, would come back to report them wiped out.

Skillful scouting supplied Carlson's Raiders with full information about the enemy's number, location of bases and the Jap garrisons' fire power. When they eventually turned back on their own lines, they had more than four hundred Japs to their credit and brought back a complete report of the enemy's strength and dispositions. More important, they had given the Japs a much-needed shaking up.

Young Richard McCallister, a Marine private first class from Leipsic, Ohio, had an exciting experience about this time. He was having a swim in the surf off Lunga, near a small supply ship which was unloading offshore, a little further out. The day was beautiful; a strange peace and quiet enveloped the landscape. McCallister's watchful gaze focused on and followed a moving, finely drawn white line, scratching the otherwise unruffled surface of the mirror-smooth water. A periscope rose near the cargo vessel. A second later he spied the wake of a torpedo racing toward the ship. Fascinated, he watched it miss the stern by a few feet and head straight for him. He turned over like a seal and made for shore, setting an all-time record. Before he reached land the 2000-pound missile flashed past him about three feet away and slithered up on the sand. McCallister swears he broke all sprint records as he legged it away from the torpedo, which he feared might have been set to destroy itself. As it happened, the thing didn't explode and our Navy technicians had ample opportunity to examine it carefully for possible innovations.

On November 2, a Marine patrol of forty men was sent across the island of Malaita to wipe out a small number of Japs who were established comfortably in the buildings of copra exporters, whose white plantation managers and overseers had been evacuated. About twenty-two Japanese occupied the northern tip of the island, which was about a hundred and ten miles long and twenty miles wide. From this tip, they radioed information of our movements on Guadalcanal to their headquarters.

Major Donald W. Fuller, of Harland, Maine, planned the expedition, but at the last minute was assigned elsewhere, leaving Lieutenant J. Wendell Crain of Ada, Oklahoma, in charge. With the Marines went Lieutenant Robert Adams, of San Diego, California, from the Marine medical corps, and a Navy hospital corpsman.

They embarked in two small launches from Tulagi, crossed sixty miles of rough sea and landed about twenty-four miles from narrow Cape Astrolobe on the northwestern tip of Malaita, where they bivouacked. Americans were still voting in the 1942 elections when the invaders split into six teams; each man was familiarized with the part he was to play.

At five-thirty that afternoon they set out on a march over trackless undergrowth and rugged terrain. They pushed ahead as rapidly as the country allowed, and at 5:30 A.M. reached their objective. Lieutenant Crain narrates: "It was getting light when the six teams encircled three sides of the enemy camp. The ocean was on the fourth side, so there was no way for the Japs to escape. The camp was in a small clearing on the coastal road built by the former British plantation people. There were four open-sided shacks. A mess hall, a galley and a storehouse were along the road. The wireless shack was situated a few yards away.

"My team crawled to within fifteen yards of the mess hall. We watched the Japs walk around, wash up and brush their teeth, getting ready for chow. At 7:45 A.M. fourteen of them were in the mess hall, eating native potatoes and bananas, and drinking coffee. We had hoped to get all twenty-two together, but when two of the fourteen prepared to leave, I decided to give the signal to commence firing.

"A corporal in my team had a tommy gun and the others used automatic rifles and Springfields. We got every one of the fourteen in the mess hall. All the others were killed near by. Three had walked down toward the river; two of them were killed, the third was wounded and ran into the bush. Two were down on the beach. One was wounded and surrendered when he saw his companion killed. The rest were just outside the mess hall. One made a break for the radio shack, probably to try to send a message, but took only about three steps before he went down.

"It was all over in five minutes. The enemy didn't fire a single shot. The attack was too sudden. The one Jap we brought back, a big lad, wouldn't talk much because he was scared almost to death.

"The natives were overjoyed at our success because the Japs had been living off their gardens and stealing their chickens. The natives gave us plenty of fruit and sang a lot of native songs for us. Before we left we had them all singing the Marine Hymn."

The aviation units on Henderson Field were under the command of Major General Roy S. Geiger, USMC. Every bit an airman, his past performances in aviation and day-to-day performance in the air had stamped him as a fighting personality and had placed him high in the ranks. He set the men a fine example by his unconcern in the face of danger, his alertness and his wise decisions.

Commanding an air squadron in France, Geiger won his first Navy Cross for heroism during the first World War. When the Navy began to stress instrument flying in 1927, and issued a syllabus on the subject, General Geiger called in his aide, Toby Munn (or so the story goes), and asked him what this new fangled business was all about. Munn explained that the new school of thought held that the old seat-of-the-pants method of flying was inferior, that pilots should fly by instruments. Geiger is said to have replied: "Well, I've been flying for twenty years without it, but there is probably something to it, so we'll test it out."

For days the general studied all the notes that were available on the subject, and plunged himself deeply into technical literature. At last, satisfied that he had it straight, he sent for Toby Munn once more, and inquired: "Is this all there is to it?" When Munn replied that, apparently, there was nothing more, the general told him to keep track of the weather and let him know the first day that visibility was low over an extended area.

There came a day when the ceiling was zero-zero all along the seaboard. Toby Munn reported. General Geiger climbed into his plane and flew on instruments through the soup from Quantico, Virginia, to Miami. When he stepped out of his machine, he remarked: "There's really nothing to it. Seem to have been doing it all my life."

For his personal use at Guadalcanal, General Geiger had a Catalina at his disposal which was flown by Major Jack Cramm, with whom he had been associated for many years. Tireless Geiger would often insist on taking off to search the seas for Jap vessels. He is known to have spent all night in his PBY, shadowing Jap convoys.

One afternoon Major Cramm arrived late from a flight and set the general's Catalina down on the field. That night the Japs began an intensive bombardment of the American positions. Sitting out the shelling in the same foxhole with Cramm, the general demonstrated great concern for the safety of his craft and berated his friend for setting the machine down where it might be destroyed.

The following morning, when an early scout reported an enemy transport unloading supplies off Cape Esperance, the general called Cramm and told him that, since the Catalina was here, he might as well load her up with torpedoes and join the boys in getting that transport. The major was more than eager. As soon as the armament crew had fitted a pair of torpedoes to the slings, he took off. Waiting until the dive bombers started down, he brought the big slow-flying plane in and launched his fish, scoring one hit. Undoubtedly it helped send the ship to the bottom. A few minutes later he returned to the airdrome, flying very low, actually brushing the tops of the coconut palms to get away from four Zeros which buzzed angrily around the big plane, trying desperately to shoot it down.

When General Geiger first arrived at Guadalcanal the enemy was sending over as many as 150 to 200 planes daily. By comparison, we had a ridiculously small number of aircraft and were able to maintain these few only with great difficulty. One morning Geiger awoke to find a squadron of Zeros patrolling the air overhead; he ordered eight Grumman Wildcats aloft to drive them away. Evidently the enemy pilots were confident they could handle the small American formation, because they passed up the chance to riddle our planes in the take-off. Instead, they waited until our fliers had climbed to 7000 feet before attacking. That was a serious mistake. At the end of the day Marine fighters had accounted for twenty Zeros against the loss of five Wildcats. Three of our pilots were rescued.

That battle was the first major engagement of Marine squadron VF-121, commanded by Duke Davis, of which Joe Foss, who has twenty-six Jap planes to his credit, was a member. Incomparable Lieutenant Colonel Joe Bauer was the squadron's air officer and Major Walt Bayler, the last man off Wake Island, was fighter director. When two hundred Jap machines came over the following day, the squadron collected twenty-two Zeros and eight bombers. Four days later, only eight of the original twenty-seven American fighter planes brought in were still able to fly. It was a small price to pay, considering the damage inflicted on the Japs.

Although the Japanese were making it tough going, our scanty force on Guadalcanal put all the pressure it could on the enemy. As one of our troops there remarked: "If the Nips can keep from crying, we'll do the best we can to stop them from laughing."

With their few planes they struck out at Japanese positions, ships and bases through the whole Solomons area. Fortresses aided in the assault, Navy dive bombers worked on the Jap shore positions, and day after day Army pilots in their Airacobras carried out low bombing and strafing attacks.

Every flier who ever served on Guadalcanal speaks in high terms of those Army men, who took their Airacobras and P-40 pursuit planes over enemy positions several times daily, as long as there was ammunition and their machines held out. Working at treetop level, they were easy prey for every Jap rifle, machine gun and small anti-aircraft weapon. And there was little glory. Theirs was not the high-flying fighting and dueling for enemy scalps, which brings fame and decorations. It was a dangerous task with the certainty of a fatal crack-up if their engine was hit or quit of its own accord. Hedgehopping and flying close to the ground does not provide the essential air space to glide back safely to the airfield if the power is off, or to set the plane down on a level stretch and leg it home, or to hit the silk and float down.

These fliers seldom get mention, much less see their names splashed across newspapers, yet their contribution in bringing flying machine guns down to point-blank range, the better to lash out at the enemy, is of utmost importance. Their task is much like that of a tank crew's, without the armor to protect them against hostile fire.

November 3 saw the American troops chalk up a day's bag of 350 Japs killed and three 75-mm. field guns, twelve 37-mm. guns and thirty machine guns captured, and that night, American fleet units shelled the enemy positions near Kokumbona.

Next day reinforcements arrived to relieve our battle-weary Marine and Army units. From the heights beyond the airfield, the Japs sprayed the landing beach with gunfire, but they did no appreciable damage. The new arrivals quickly and methodically established themselves, even as small boats shuttled back and forth busily, unloading the anchored vessels in a race against the clock. They intended to be away before dark. Twice that day enemy bombers were reported approaching, causing an interruption in the unloading. Each time the ships moved out to sea, where they could maneuver, while American aircraft went aloft and turned the enemy back.

At night, when the Japs launched their customary counterattack, they were repulsed strongly. Our forces were becoming powerful. We were gaining a firmer foothold with each new shipment of men and supplies, and consequently we were beginning to hit back more heavily.

From Henderson Field, American daylight scouts kept a constant watch over the Solomons for a distance of two hundred miles to the north, northwest and west. When two of the scouts who flew reconnaissance over Santa Isabel failed to return, the Marines decided to take over and crack down on Rekata Bay in a surprise raid.

Members of Marine fighter squadron VF-212 took part in the action. This squadron was never officially based on Henderson Field. Its members delivered fighter planes to the island and joined any action that was executed while they were on Guadalcanal, waiting for a troop plane to return them to their own base, several hundred miles distant. Their scoreboard showed ninety-four Jap aircraft downed and two destroyers sunk.

Long before daylight eight Marine pilots took off from Henderson and flew to the northwest into the night. They would arrive over their target about an hour before dawn. Lieutenant (now Captain) Robert Stout, of Fort Laramie, Wyoming, was among the fliers. It was still quite dark when they reached their destination. They doused their lights, which had been kept on during the flight to enable the pilots to keep formation. As they selected targets for their bombs and machine guns, the Japs began to send up an appreciable anti-aircraft barrage. Some Jap planes rose to the sky. The Marine formation dropped lower for a better look at the beach. Stout noticed several phosphorescent streaks race across the inky waters of the bay; they were float planes taking off. He led his men in a slanting dive, machine-gunning the dark blurs in front of the faintly gleaming foam. Two were destroyed. Other planes in Stout's formation bombed fuel dumps, buildings and planes hauled up on the sand.

Stout saw two aircraft fly across his bow, suddenly, with navigation lights burning. The second plane made a shallow dive onto the tail of the first machine. Spotting it as a Jap lined up one of his Wildcats, Stout radioed a warning to the pilot and nosed over to attack the Jap machine. A second or two before he was within shooting distance, he saw tracer bullets leap from the bow of the rear aircraft and blaze a fiery trail into the fuselage of the lead plane. It disintegrated before his eyes. At almost the same moment Stout lined up his enemy and gave him a long burst which sent the float plane crashing away into oblivion.

With the bombs dropped according to plan, and the machine-gun ammunition expended on the general camp area, the fliers turned back toward base. Their mission was completed.

Stout felt badly as he flew home. He couldn't stop thinking of the comrade whom he hadn't been able to reach in time. He still didn't know who it was, and would not know until the flight landed and he counted noses. Henderson Field came into view. It was now daylight. Stout landed, leaped out of his plane and discovered two others had come in before him. The three Marines watched the stragglers circle to land, one at a time, and identified the individual fliers overhead by the numbers on their Wildcats. Eight planes had left and five . . . six . . . seven were back. They were about to turn away, knowing now who it was that was left behind, when there was the roar of another engine. Over the treetops came the blunt nose of a Wildcat. It circled low. Stout and his squadron mates watched breathlessly. Then there was a yell.

One of the boys had recognized the number before the others, and it was the missing man.

What they had thought was their own plane diving into the bay was actually one Jap shooting down another! Seconds later, of course, the unwitting Jap had been shot down by Stout.

Japan, her forces again re-formed and plans revised, was now about to unleash another powerful drive for the recovery of Guadalcanal. Our long-distance aerial patrols were beginning to report fresh concentrations of Jap warships in the New Britain-northern Solomons region and our Navy calmly set its countermoves in motion. The wheels were running smoothly by the time the Jap ships slipped their cables to steam south. The hostile force consisted of three units: a convoy of eight transports and five supply vessels, guarded by cruisers and destroyers; a fleet of two battleships, cruisers and destroyers; and a group of ships similar to the second unit. The spearhead of the Jap force consisted of two *Kongo* class (29,330-ton) battleships, two heavy cruisers, four light cruisers and ten destroyers.

Unknown to this expeditionary force, an American fleet of notable strength was poised to strike.

November 10, the Marine Corps' 167th birthday, was an occasion warranting celebration, and the Reapers, on their secluded little island, were happy to participate. Celebrations began the day before, when everyone congregated for a festive dinner.

Bobby Edwards and Ed Polson thought a deer hunt would see the day in fittingly, and so they set out for the hills, armed with rifles and flashlights. They bagged three deer and loaded them onto their jeep. Rocking along toward home, Bobby was tossed off his precarious seat on the folded hood when their jeep went into a ditch. He fell on jagged rocks and cracked his kneecap.

Four Jap transports, hit by American surface vessels and aircraft, lie beached and burning at Tassafaronga after the action of November 13th and 14th, 1942.
(Official U. S. Navy Photo)

Lunga Island, Jap base in the Solomons, was desolated by an attack from American bombers on October 17, 1942. (*Official U.S. Navy Photo*)

Some of the Reapers were still celebrating when a messenger handed Commander Flatley a signal. It was the order for all fliers to man their planes and land aboard the *Enterprise* shortly after dawn. There were rounds of warm but hurried farewells before they left for camp, where the boys packed and stowed their heavy gear, including the three deer which meanwhile had been dressed. All this was sent aboard the carrier by boat. The fliers' light gear was stowed into their Wildcats.

Before dawn Flatley called the roll and gave last-minute flight instructions. Edwards, whose knee was swollen like a football, had contrived somehow to get into his plane. He had to be lifted out and hospitalized, in spite of his pleas to go along.

Finally the Reapers flew seaward to their rendezvous point, and once again set their planes down on the flight deck. It felt good to be back aboard, and the men's healthy faces, beaming with confidence, had a heartening effect on the ship's personnel.

On November 10, reconnaissance reports indicated that a big show was in the offing. The fleet kept inside a watchful screen of long-distance flying scouts who combed every square mile of the surrounding ocean for possible Jap vessels, while the Reapers flew day-long combat patrols overhead.

On the morning of Armistice Day a sizable force of American warships and supply vessels, including the new cruisers *Atlanta* and *Juneau*, and Rear Admiral Daniel J. Callaghan's flagship, the cruiser *San Francisco*, arrived at Guadalcanal, with sorely needed material. Their coming signaled an increase in hostile air activity, but the Japs had little success.

Warships guarded the transports while they disgorged their supplies. Early on November 12, Marine and Army artillery officers went aboard the warships. Those officers well acquainted with the territory pointed out the Jap areas best suited for a going-over with high explosive shells. The

ships strung out in column and steamed to the west. Abeam
of Point Cruz, they poured 8-inch, 5-inch, 20-mm. shells and
even machine-gun bullets into Japanese army positions and
supply dumps among the trees.

A single Airacobra circled above the various targets and
from time to time radioed "target demolished," whereupon
the vessels moved majestically ahead to devastate the next
sector. They knocked out a Jap base at Kokumbona and
destroyed landing barges and main supply dumps at Cape
Tassafaronga. With their task completed, they turned back
to Henderson Field.

Aboard one of the cruisers, a joyful Marine officer was
moved nearly to tears when he saw the enemy's strength demolished. He and his troops had fought the Japs laboriously
for many a day without much visible result. To see the destruction wrought upon them so simply and thoroughly now
made him want to personally thank both captain and crew.

November 12 brought a particularly heavy Jap air attack
aimed at the American ships. Twenty-seven bombers escorted
by ten Zeros came over at 11 A.M. They were ripped apart by
our fighter planes and the guns of the assembled ships. Only
seventeen bombers escaped.

That afternoon, seventeen fast, twin-engined land planes,
armed with torpedoes, made for the American transports and
warships. They were spotted a long way out, already deployed for the attack in a single line abeam. Their powerful
twin engines brought them in at a clip faster than three
hundred miles per hour. The *Juneau* and several destroyers
screened the flank from which the attack was aimed and they
opened fire with all guns. Several transports began to join in,
but they partly balked the warships' aim and effectiveness
with their high hulls, because the Jap planes approached
almost at water level.

The ships scored by concentrating their fire. The first torpedo plane sloshed into the sea. Others followed as the fire

of all ships took effect and the enemy's strength diminished rapidly. A few Wildcats entered the fight, disregarding their own anti-aircraft barrage, in their determination to shatter the attack before the enemy was within range.

Only five enemy planes remained in flight. They were too far off to aim correctly, but the Jap pilots let go their "fish." Then, in a desperate effort to escape, they weaved between the ships, hoping mistakenly that fear of hitting their own vessels would discourage the gunners from shooting.

Two Jap planes, both damaged, headed west through the gap between Savo Island and Guadalcanal. A Wildcat overtook one flying only a few feet above the water. Taking up position just over the Jap, the pilot let down his landing gear and began banging his wheels on top of the enemy machine. In a futile effort to escape his tormentor, the Jap yawed from side to side. The Wildcat stayed right with him and finally succeeded in battering the big plane lower and lower, forcing it to crash into the sea.

The destroyer *Buchanan* suffered damage and casualties in the attack, and so did the *San Francisco* when a flaming Jap plane smashed into the cruiser's after superstructure and exploded before sliding overboard. This unfortunate accident killed thirty of the *San Francisco's* crew and injured several others.

Later that afternoon reconnaissance reported the approach of two or three Jap battleships, some heavy and light cruisers, and probably ten destroyers. They were expected to arrive about midnight. Admiral Callaghan hurried the unloading, and shortly after dark, shepherded the transports safely out of Savo Sound and to sea. Then the cruiser force returned to Guadalcanal to await the enemy.

Midnight had passed and the first hour of the new day, November 13, had ticked off when our warships off Kokumbona Point got the first contact report. The Japanese force came up in three loose columns. Two entered through the north channel, between Savo and Tulagi, while the third approached the southern channel. The American force, consisting of four cruisers, including the *San Francisco* and *Atlanta,* and a flotilla of destroyers, was headed for the south of Savo, where it could steam inside the Jap southern and northern columns.

The enemy outnumbered Admiral Callaghan's force by about two to one, and was more heavily armored and gunned. It was an unequal line-up, and on paper, almost certain annihilation faced the American force.

Although ready and about to open fire, taut crewmen jumped when the nearest Jap cruiser switched her searchlights on the *Atlanta,* cutting the night with a stark white light which bathed the cruiser.

Instantly Lieutenant Commander Lloyd M. Austin, the *Atlanta's* gunnery officer, ordered: "Action port! Illuminating ship is target. Open fire!" The *Atlanta's* guns roared a split second before the Jap fired, and while her muzzles spouted flame, the *San Francisco* opened with her first salvo.

Engaging the illuminating cruiser with her 5-inch guns, she swung her 8-inch rifles back to blast a Jap destroyer off the seas. This vessel had hauled around for a sneak torpedo attack on her disengaged side, but was detected by alert spotters and literally torn to pieces by half a dozen 250-pound projectiles. Having cleared her quarter of this menace, her turrets swung back for a rapid pounding of the initial target. The enemy's fire was high, ripping into the *Atlanta's* superstructure. The tremendous blast caused by the heavy projectiles scattered fragments of shell casing and jagged splinters of wrecked armor plate everywhere. Rear Admiral Norman Scott was killed during the first ninety seconds. The navigator, Lieutenant Commander J. S. Smith, Jr., was mortally wounded and Captain S. P. Jenkins sustained leg injuries.

Our destroyers moved in and sent their torpedoes against the hostile hulls. The little *Cushing* (*Mahan* class, 1500 tons, commissioned 1936) had been struck early and lay dead in the water between two enemy columns. Although surrounded by Jap vessels, her skipper ordered the torpedo tubes trained on the belly of a Jap heavyweight which loomed out of the darkness. Every time this battle wagon fired her batteries, tongues of flame from the 14-inch gun muzzles illuminated her towering superstructure. Aided by the flashes of American shells, the *Cushing* set her tubes and unleashed a broadside of four torpedos at almost point-blank range. Two of these struck and exploded close to the under-water hull of the giant. The *Cushing* turned her attention to the second Jap column, and as fast as the torpedoes could be loaded into the tubes, they were loosed at the Jap ships until her stock was exhausted. The *Cushing's* torpedoes struck home. Disabled and drifting, she scored hits on four Japanese warships. Struck again and again, the gallant little fighter's guns spat destruction while water poured in and flooded her magazines. Shooting, she went to her grave.

Ships were burning on all sides. Our destoyers had been hit hard and flames licked from the *Atlanta's* forward superstructure. She was outlined plainly and drew fire from all types of guns.

Suddenly she rose, lifted by two violent torpedo explosions. They tore gaping holes in her steel plates below the water line and smashed some machinery. Her big guns ceased functioning. The electric power, which swings the turrets, had been cut off and the emergency hand-operated equipment had been wrecked. She veered out of line and soon floated dead on the sea, ablaze.

Taking over the brunt of the battle, the *San Francisco* steamed past regally, her guns flashing defiance. She was followed by her light cruisers and the surviving destroyers, all presenting an unforgettable picture as they moved down the Japanese lines, firing every gun as fast as the weapons could be loaded, aimed and the firing button pressed. All the ships armed with torpedo tubes launched their "fish" and soon the sea was crisscrossed with white wakes.

Admiral Callaghan's ships were hitting with full power at close range, and they were hitting often. Another, and yet another, enemy ship would give up trying to stay afloat and keel over, or simply dip her stern and slide beneath the surface.

No sea action had been fought at such close quarters since the invention of high-power guns, and the tars hit with every-thing they had. It was the greatest slugging match of all modern naval warfare, and as yet, no one could pick the winner. It appeared that the decision would go to the last ship afloat.

After her consort, the destroyer *Cushing*, had been disabled, the *Laffey*, under Lieutenant Commander W. E. Hank, filled the breach and steamed up to a Japanese battleship whose great fighting tops dwarfed her own small hull. She fired a span of torpedoes into the giant. Then, almost scraping across the Jap's bow and clearing it by a bare few yards, the little destroyer fired not only her quick-shooting 5-inch guns into her giant opponent, but her batteries of 20-mm. automatic cannon and .50-caliber machine guns, raking the Jap's bridge and forward superstructure. So close were these two vessels that the *Laffey's* officers fired pistols at Jap sailors manning their posts on the pagodalike control tower. This had not been done since the days of sail and grappling irons.

Past the battleship the *Laffey* churned close beside a cruiser and swept this enemy vessel with fire from all her weapons. As the cruiser passed into the night the *Laffey* emerged into a sea brightly illuminated by flaming ships. She found herself amid the enemy force and became the target of concentrated fire. A salvo from the big rifles of a Jap heavyweight struck and finished the brave vessel. But never before had two de-stroyers been so deadly with their light weapons as had the *Cushing* and *Laffey*.

From the beaches and elevations of Guadalcanal, the Marines watched the battle grow in intensity until it reached a crescendo of fiery destruction. They saw the warships pass through the enemy line and saw the engagement break up into gun duels between single ships and groups of vessels. They saw the sky alight with the brillance of magnesium flares and saw warships go to flaming deaths. They saw clouds of hissing steam and vapor sheath other vessels. Volleys of white-hot steel and blazing debris marked those about to go down. Above it all, the lazily descending flares bobbed in the air, suspended from their parachutes by long cords, lighting friend and foe to doom.

When it appeared that the smaller American force must be at the mercy of the enemy, the Japs lost heart. They were totally broken up and no longer held any kind of formation. Possibly they had very little idea of what ships had been lost, and probably no idea of the extremely small fleet opposing them. Extremely nervous, they no longer trusted any ship and fired at every shape looming through the uncertain light, including their own vessels. Knowing they had been hit hard, they decided to withdraw, and turned away without accomplishing their mission and without destroying aircraft or American positions on Guadalcanal. One after the other they slid seaward, headed back to base. Their transports, which had followed them two hours or so astern, executed an about-turn and fled for safety. The sporadic gunfire became less distinct as they drew off and soon Savo Sound was silent—silent except for the crackling flames and explosions aboard the stricken vessels. Three of them were enemy warships which only twenty-five minutes before had been sound and effective fighting mechanisms. Now they were sinking hulks, torn by torpedoes, shells and explosions. The engagement had been short, but it had been waged with a ferocity never before experienced in naval battle.

Doctors and hospital corpsmen had more wounded to treat

than there had been in a single engagement since the days of John Paul Jones. In the engine rooms and lower compartments of the damaged warships the black gangs and damage repair crews labored to shore up holes, pump out water and strengthen the bulkheads.

The gunners helped tend their wounded, moved their dead comrades aside, cleaned guns and stacked· ammunition in preparation for more shooting to come.

Destroyers and smaller Higgins boats searched the sea for survivors, many of whom clung to rafts. Others floated in their life jackets. Once aboard the ships, many of the rescued pitched in and helped to make the damaged vessels shipshape.

When dawn came at last the men aboard the stricken *Atlanta* saw the dim silhouette of a destroyer lying straight ahead, obviously disabled. Closer scrutiny identified the vessel as a Jap whose crew was busy about the deck. Unable to do anything herself, the *Atlanta* signaled to another near-by cruiser, which swung her 8-inch gun turrets and steadied for the gun pointers to line up the enemy carefully. With well-spaced, deep and resounding volleys, another Jap was sent to Iron Bottom Bay.

This ended the first phase of the Battle for Guadalcanal, which was to continue for another two days and nights. Admiral Callaghan's cruiser force, though greatly outnumbered, had proved more than a match for Hirohito's vaunted battleship spearhead. A tabulation showed that the guns of the comparatively small American force had wrecked a battleship and sunk three cruisers and several destroyers. Our losses included the cruiser *Juneau* and some destroyers, and the *Atlanta* was left mortally damaged.

Admiral Callaghan paid with his life for this victory. The same explosion also killed Captain Cassin Young, the *San Francisco's* executive officer, Commander Mark Crouter and Commander Hubbard, and severely wounded Commander

Rae Arison, the navigation officer. Commander Herbert Schonland, next ranking officer, busy below with damage control, asked Lieutenant Commander Bruce McCandless, Jr., to take command of the bridge. McCandless kept the ship on her course and the crew carried on.

On the *Atlanta* it became obvious shortly after midday that the crew's untiring effort to save her was in vain. All except a handful of men were ordered to abandon ship and were transferred ashore in landing craft. Only a demolition party, commanded by Captain Jenkins, remained. Lieutenant Commander John T. Wulff and an assistant attended to the opening of the ship's sea cocks and watertight doors to allow the inrushing sea to flood the hull. Then the six men stationed themselves forward in the bow of the ship. Wulff held the plunger that would fire an explosive charge planted inside the hull. The captain gave the nod and Wulff shoved down the plunger. There was a dull booming as her plates gave way and the Atlanta began to sink. Captain Jenkins stood aside as the others filed over the rail and into the waiting boat. He followed, the last man to leave the ship. They watched the waves fold over her. Then the captain ordered the small boat to head for Guadalcanal.

The *Enterprise,* too, was headed for Guadalcanal. At daybreak nine of her torpedo planes, led by Lieutenant Commander Albert P. ("Scoffer") Coffin, and escorted by six Reapers under Lieutenant John Sutherland, winged toward the island. Their orders had been to report and attack hostile ships en route.

Slightly before the "Moppers Up," or Buzzard Brigade (as Torpedo Squadron 10 was called variously) took off, Swede Vejtasa and three fellow Reapers had been launched for combat patrol. During the morning they had sighted a Kawanishi on the hunt for American warships. Led by Swede, the fighters came up for the attack rapidly. Swede struck from above and one side and riddled the big machine with a burst from his machine guns. He was followed closely by his wing man, who added a few seconds' fire from his bank of .50s, then, as an added flourish, exploded his ammunition in the bow gunner's compartment. With its gunners killed and its engine spraying gasoline, the machine burst into flame, scattering wings and fuselage over the sky before the scout had seen or reported the size and strength of the American task force.

Scoffer Coffin's TBFs (Avengers), with a mop-swinging figure painted on the fuselage of each machine, meanwhile had reached and rounded the eastern cape of Guadalcanal. Whoops of joy went up at sight of a crippled Japanese battleship ahead. Her hull was ripped and her machinery knocked out, but some of her armament was still in working order. She moved inside a screen of destroyers ten miles off Savo Island at a speed of about five knots. The Buzzards wasted no time getting to work. Jap warships were their business. To distract some of the enemy gunfire, Sutherland, split the Reapers into pairs, led them high above the Jap ship, and when Scoffer gave the word that his torpedo planes were in position and about to begin their attack run, the Reapers, too, nosed over and dived. This led the enemy gunners to believe they were being attacked by dive bombers as well as torpedo planes, and caused them to distribute their fire both high and low among the attacking planes. They hit none. The Buzzards came in through the anti-aircraft curtain and loosed their torpedoes. Two exploded against the battleship's hull. The Reapers, meanwhile, had dropped to 1500 feet and attacked the Jap sailors on the decks and the ship's upper works.

The big *Kongo* class battleship was taking her full share of punishment. She took an estimated eleven torpedoes and six or seven bombs before she was in serious enough condition to be scuttled.

After this blitz the mopping-up Buzzards and six Reapers re-formed and headed for Henderson Field, where they reported to Brigadier General Louis Wood, USMC, in command of the squadrons based at the field. It was General Wood who uttered the immortal words: "I used to be a kindly old colonel, but I sure am a bloodthirsty general now."

The Reapers encountered their old friends Ensigns William ("Whitey") Noll, H. B. ("Dusty") Miller, and Lieutenants L. C. Lew and R. F. ("Pete") Daggett. Noll volunteered information about the island and brought them up to date on the events there. He kept them amused with numerous stories. Miller, he related, had been souvenir hunting one day with three well-experienced Marines and, as an afterthought, had brought a rifle. Trekking along the quiet jungle paths, one of the Marines would snatch Miller's rifle before he could even think about it and fire into the undergrowth, each time killing a concealed Jap. They got six in all, without once giving poor Dusty a chance to use his own gun.

Then there was the story of "Pistol Pete" and "Millimeter Mike," the Jap guns hidden in the slopes beyond the airfield. With clocklike regularity they announced the end and beginning of each new day with a few nuisance volleys. In the same class was "Maytag Charlie," with his rasping, machine-like rattletrap plane, who flew over almost daily, paying regular nuisance visits. More fantastic than these were the mysterious workings of "Oscar," the Jap sub with the playful habit of surfacing offshore at night to fire nuisance rounds of shells onto the beach.

With the late afternoon report of a strong force of Jap warships moving into Guadalcanal, the garrison prepared for another night's shelling. Sutherland, who thought it a good idea to get some sleep first, preferred a comfortable bed in a tent near the airfield to the proffered front-line foxhole. Furthest away from the airfield, the front line had long been recognized by veteran Guadalcanalians as the safest place.

Scarcely had Sutherland dropped off to sleep when one of the fiercest naval attacks on Henderson Field began.

The first salvo woke him. He rolled over and was going back to sleep when he realized that this was serious business. He scurried for the nearest foxhole. Next morning he discovered how wise a course he had followed; there were only shell fragments where his bed had been.

The three other Reapers, still listening to Whitey Noll's tales when the first shell exploded, ran for the dugouts near the gun positions. These were considered choice locations because the cannoneers had built them deep and roofed them over with logs and bags of soil. As they reached the first dugout a voice called out from the dark entrance: "Can't get in here, bud, it's full." But the second offered them shelter. "Come over here. There's plenty of room," someone in it called out. The four turned and ran toward it; the man in front dived for the entrance. While he was in mid-air, the same voice shouted: "Careful! There's a foot of water on the floor!" Too late. The victim landed on all fours, hugging the mud. The others entered more carefully. A candle sputtered in one corner. By its light they made out the form of Captain Jerry Russel (USMC artillery). The captain identified the reverberating thunder of each gun. As the sound penetrated to the dugout, he would remark: "That's a Hypo battery" (Marine 11th battery, 75-mm.), or "That's Easy battery . . . ragged shooting . . . That's the 105s . . . They're good stuff. . . . That's the new 155-mm. rifle . . . just got it mounted, an excellent piece . . . That's a Jap 14-inch shell. . . ."

Meanwhile, the Reapers gave Whitey Noll reproachful glances. He had assured them only a few minutes before that they scarcely ever were shelled any more.

Outside the night was heavy with battle din. Coconut palms fell like matchsticks, mounds of earth formed around mouths of craters, and whining missiles cut through the air, ripping into the soil, wounding and sometimes killing.

The enemy's purpose was twofold: to destroy our planes and to soften up our defenses and fighting men. The attack was severe. In addition to the 250-pound shells from the heavy cruisers, there had been many 1460-pound projectiles from the battleships, and all of them had been exploding somewhere within the target area.

In the midst of the Jap attack half a dozen small, fast, plywood PT boats, each armed with four torpedoes, closed with the enemy in the dark. Their six-man crews fired from close range and scored hits on a cruiser and destroyer. Uncertain of the strength of the attackers, and mindful of their surprise the previous night, the enemy retired. As suddenly as it began, the shelling stopped and the hostile force disappeared in the direction of Savo Island.

After the bombardment ceased, the Reapers got some sleep at last. They were awakened early on November 14 by the morning stand-to. Expecting to find few of the planes in navigable shape after the terrific night bombardment, they were amazed when a tour of the field disclosed that several aircraft had been damaged by blasts and shell fragments, but the skilled ground crews had made repairs and readied most of them for the day's work.

Pre-dawn scouts had radioed contact with thirteen Jap transports about a hundred and seventy-five miles off the island. Laden with 25,000 to 30,000 troops and great quantities of weapons and supplies, these vessels were intended to strengthen Jap positions on Guadalcanal. Other air scouts reported hostile warships in a second formation, also steaming for Guadalcanal. Their position was given as midway between Vangunu Island and Santa Isabel. From a third point, to the north, a powerful Japanese battleship fleet was reported. Unless an unusually strong American naval force appeared from somewhere, the situation would be critical.

The men on Guadalcanal did not know the whereabouts of the American fleet, nor did the Japanese. Actually, Admiral William F. Halsey was in the area, and in force, but like the skilled fighter he is, he was playing his cards close to his chest, luring the Japs into a trap. He kept his strength well out of sight of land to the south of Guadalcanal and maintained an aerial fighter screen to prevent hostile patrol planes from getting through.

To sink the transports before they reached the island, our Army, Navy and Marine bomber and torpedo planes went after the "soft-skinned" vessels, which were covered solidly with umbrellas of Zeros from near-by bases. Every time our planes came close the fighters met heavy opposition, and before the day was far advanced both air forces were locked in hot battle. The air combats occurred in waves, every new formation of American planes starting fresh conflagrations. The sky was laced with wisps of smoke in machine-gun-created patterns. Occasional flaming planes and black gun-bursts marred the design.

Although the Jap airmen fought well, American bombs and torpedoes went on crashing into the convoy, and as the day wore on the decreasing enemy force, steaming ever southward, left larger numbers of stricken vessels lagging behind. The path of the enemy could be traced across the sea by the flotsam cast off from ships already gone down or crippled and adrift. Bombs and torpedoes had killed or wounded hundreds aboard the packed vessels, and the troops who had thronged topside, fearful of being trapped in the lower flats, had been killed off by machine guns like swarms of flies.

The *Enterprise's* northward course had brought the enemy armada well within range of her air attack group. At 8:30 A.M., on November 14, word had been received that a large formation of unidentified planes was approaching from the north. This incorrect report precipitated the launching of sixteen dive bombers with a Reaper escort of ten Wildcats.

The planes had orders to fly northward and to expect more definite orders later.

The dive bombers divided into three sections. The first was led by Lieutenant Commander Bucky Lee, squadron commander; the second by VBD-10 skipper Lieutenant Commander Alfred Thomas, and the third by Lieutenant Bernie Strong of SBD-10. Reaper Leader Flatley headed the escort.

They flew on their search course, listening for radio directions. Their order to swing to a definite target would come through as soon as the scouts, who had been launched earlier, contacted the enemy. As the formation passed the Russel Islands, a pair of float-type Jap fighters put in an appearance and were all set to attack the bombers. Seeing the Wildcats, they dived and flew for safety like badly scared birds.

When the Wildcats reached the limit of their range without a contact report coming through, Flatley adhered to the original orders and led his Reapers back to the carrier. Bucky Lee and his cohorts continued on alone.

The *Enterprise* scouts, not quite a hundred miles ahead of this formation, meanwhile made contact with and engaged the Japanese transports. Lieutenant Robert ("Hoot") Gibson, of Unionville, Missouri, and R. M. Buchanan sighted the enemy past New Georgia Island. Clifford Schimdele, Gibson's rear gunner, radioed the force's position, course, speed, number and types. Hoot and Buchanan then continued their search for bigger game.

Gibson reports: "We were seeking the main enemy fleet, which was believed to be lurking somewhere in this area. After passing around the southwestern end of New Georgia, we sighted a force of six cruisers and five destroyers. The cruisers steamed in two columns of three ships each. There were a lot of broken clouds. After making the initial contact report, we continued the search in the hope of locating a flat-top.

"We searched for forty-five minutes. The hostile ships fired at us whenever we passed within range and we made use of the broken clouds to make it awkward for the gunners to get a good shot at our planes. Since we'd been ordered to await an acknowledgment of our contact report before attacking or leaving any enemy force, we idled around. Later, I discovered that the carrier had been trying to reach me, but that my receiver had gone haywire and I couldn't pick up the signal.

"After about an hour of this, our gasoline was getting dangerously low, so Buchanan and I decided to climb for diving altitude and attack the cruiser force below. When we got into position, we waited for a favorable cloud break. Then we let down, with our noses pointed right at the biggest cruiser, a heavy of the *Nati* class. From training and experience, I knew how difficult it is for gunners to hit a dive bomber coming down almost directly from above, and though I didn't like the heavy anti-aircraft guns, I didn't worry much about them while we were diving from the 12,000 to the 6000-foot section. But once we passed below that level and into range of the light automatics, it got dangerous enough.

"The size of the victim grew in the sights until I could see its deck clearly. When my altimeter registered 1000 feet, I squeezed the bomb release lever and the 1000-pounder fell away. Then I pulled out of the dive and began to retire.

"Buchanan was right astern and let his bomb go a couple of seconds later. Schimdele, who was shooting his machine guns into the cruiser as I pulled away, saw our bomb hit and erupt violently on the starboard side, right amidships. The shock of the explosion seemed to jerk the cruiser violently. Buchanan's bomb exploded slightly abaft amidships, on the port side.

Aerial view of hotly contested Lunga Airport, Guadalcanal Island, taken after our Marines had driven out the Japs. The almost completed runway is shown, and (upper right) the circular dispersal area. (*Official U. S. Navy Photo*)

These are the men of Bombing-Ten, who worked with the Reapers. Pilots, radiomen and ground crews are shown lined up under the coconut palms at an advanced Pacific base, where they landed from their carrier for relaxation ashore. (*Official U. S. Navy Photo*)

"My gunner switched from his machine guns to his camera and took about two hundred feet of film of the mounting fire aboard the cruiser as we withdrew."

I questioned Hoot about the length of time he figured he was being shot at while making the attack.

"The actual dive takes no more than twenty seconds," he explained, "but they are a long twenty seconds for the pilot and radioman. Getting away takes longer still. Usually we don't steer directly away from the ship because that would give the gunners an easy shot at us. In this particular case we didn't have to worry about the victim's fire because every gun stopped shooting immediately when our bombs exploded. But this did not prevent the other ships from shooting at us. I steered a course roughly slanting, and occasionally zigzagging, to make the shot more difficult. Within perhaps fifteen seconds, we were out of the Jap's small-arms fire, but their heavies continued to shoot for perhaps half a minute.

"Buchanan's plane was damaged by a close shell burst which wrecked his rudder controls and did other damage, but he was able to maintain it in flight.

"Our fuel was rapidly running out now. As we approached Savo Island the gauge registered zero, and for a time I was afraid we would have to make a forced landing in the sea. To top it all, I saw AA shells bursting above Henderson Field, which was under heavy bomber attack. I held the Dauntless's nose in a glide, straight for the field, and put her down. Before she ran to a stop the engine died. The tanks were dry.

"Buchanan had a very lively landing. Without rudder control, flaps or brakes, he set his machine down at the beginning of the landing strip. She raced along its full length, overran the strip and continued for a couple of hundred yards before stopping, but the plane didn't nose over nor ground-loop."

Bucky Lee and his formation, upon hearing Gibson's contact report, changed course and headed for the enemy. Two other VSB-10 pilots—Lieutenant Leonard ("Bud") Lucier, of Davenport, Iowa, and Ensign Paul Halloran—who were flying the scouting leg next to Hoot, also picked up his report and swung over to add their bombs. They arrived fifteen minutes after Hoot and Buchanan had left the scene, and saw the heavy cruiser wallowing low in the water, sinking.

Bud Lucier chose another heavy and Paul picked a light cruiser. Without preliminaries, both dived to attack, their bombs exploding on the respective targets. Hit hard by antiaircraft fire, Paul's plane was forced down some distance from the enemy force. He was lost.

Lee arrived with his formation of sixteen bombers as Bud headed for Guadalcanal. As Lieutenant Russel ("Red") Hoogerwerf of Geneseo, Illinois, describes it: "We passed across the Jap cruisers and saw one heavy listing and dead in the water and two others burning. We circled while the skipper appraised the situation, then dived to bomb."

It was lightning action and over in perhaps two minutes. Although the Jap gunners filled the air with bursting ack-ack, the Americans kept coming. Spaced a few seconds apart, they roared down, loosed their heavy bombs, flattened out and sped off. They scored five hits and left two cruisers swathed in balls of thick smoke. Three of the planes held their missiles because release mechanisms failed to operate.

One cruiser had been sunk and four or five others were damaged. The planes, low on fuel and out of ammunition, were nearer to Henderson Field than to their mother ship, and so followed out orders received in flight, proceeding to Guadalcanal, where they landed in time to take part in the destruction of the Jap transport.

Hoot Gibson had landed just as several Marine dive bombers were getting ready to take off. Of course he wanted to accompany them. Lieutenant Leonard Robinson, a squadron mate who had made a forced landing on Henderson Field, was already refueled and ready to go. In spite of the enemy raid, the ground crews braved the Jap bombs to fill Hoot's tanks, and lifted a 1000-pounder into his bomb rack. The Marines took off before this operation was quite completed, to get at the Japs now a hundred and fifty miles out. Hoot taxied to the strip hurriedly, thundered down the runway and caught up with the formation about fifty miles from the target. Gibson recounts: "I teamed up with Len Robinson and Marine Sergeant Beneke. When we were still twenty miles away from the enemy we counted twelve Jap transports steaming in three columns, with seven cruisers and destroyers protecting their flanks.

"Major Richardson (USMC), in command of our formation, split us into two groups. He led one section to attack from the south and ordered the section I was with to attack from the north. Richardson's group reached the attack point more quickly, and as we circled for position we watched them batter through the defending Zeros. They dove into the AA fire curtain, dispersed their bombs, and got at least one victim.

"By that time Jap Zeros had begun to attack our section. Len, Beneke and I selected the biggest transports, a ship about 10,000 to 12,000 tons, and went in for the kill. Some of the Zeros attempted to dive with us. One clung to Robinson's tail persistently, but Schimdele turned his guns and shot the Jap away.

"This was the easiest dive I've ever made. Below was the big juicy target, full to the bursting point with Jap troops. We were coming down from astern and the enemy ship took no evasive action whatever.

"I knew I couldn't miss and released my bomb a second ahead of Robinson. As we hauled away there were two loud explosions. Both our bombs had landed amidships. Beneke, a few seconds behind us, saw the double explosion break the transport in half."

They re-formed and returned to Henderson Field at full throttle to fuel and rearm for another attack before dark. This was one of the rare opportunities of war. Only a short hop from the airdrome the sea was filled with troop-crowded transports lacking proper protection—and the day was much too short.

Jim Flatley stayed aboard the *Enterprise* just long enough to have a quick lunch. At 2:10 P.M., forty minutes after his return from the five-hour morning flight, Jim took to the air again, leading twelve Reapers. They were assigned to escort eight VSB-10 planes, armed with 1000-pound bombs; targets were the enemy transports.

After an uneventful flight of an hour and fifty minutes they sighted the nine remaining transports and supply vessels, about sixty miles from Guadalcanal, near Santa Isabel. They were screened by five or six destroyers. Approaching at 18,000 and 22,000 feet, the bombers and fighters closed in. Each bomber marked a transport. Several Mitsubishis were in the vicinity but made no move to intercept.

The Reapers separated into three four-plane sections led by Flatley, Dave Pollock and Fritz Faulkner. The Mitsus still kept their distance. If they did not attack by the time the bombers got well into their dives, Faulkner's four-plane section would stay aloft to provide high air cover while the other eight Wildcats would go down to machine-gun the vessels.

Commander Flatley relates: "The bombers were now on their way down, their tails getting smaller. We watched the Zeros, but apparently they were still disinterested. I gave the word to Dave and his section began to let down. My section also started losing height. We descended first to

10,000 feet, drew off in pairs around a circle, and pointed our Wildcats down.

"Just before we got going the bombers reached their release point and their bombs began to hit. It was a terrible picture of destruction. Three bombs exploded on three transports and literally opened up their hulls. Three bombs fell close aboard—near enough to spring the skins of three other transports. The explosions sent hundreds of tons of water into the air, and it back-crashed onto the ships.

"All this took only split seconds and we had front-row seats from our cockpits. We could see the Jap soldiers on the open decks, as tightly packed as a football crowd in a stadium."

The Reapers opened up with their machine guns at 4000 feet and, coming in, swept the decks from bow to stern. Then they pulled out, climbed, turned, and repeated their strafing attack. Frantic Japs leaped into the sea to escape the machine-gunning and the fires which the incendiary bullets had started everywhere on their transports.

Flatley pulled out after his initial attack and clawed up to 5000 feet to make his second run on a destroyer which had closed in and was firing on the planes. He and his wing man silenced the vessel and cleared the Japs off the bridge and exposed gun mounts.

The bombers re-formed quickly after their attack and some of the Reapers took up stations above them to cover their return trip to Henderson.

As soon as the Reapers divided into small groups, the Mitsus, who until now had remained aloof, gathered to attack. Ed Coalson was "beating up" the deck of a ship with his machine guns when he was jumped by two Zeros. He saw their tracers flashing past and looped to a position above and astern of the two enemy planes to pour a stream of .50s into one. The Jap kept on flying—straight into the sea.

Faulkner's group, left alone and high in the clouds, was

subjected to a brief, single-pass attack. Ensign L. E. ("Rip") Slagle contrived to squirt one Zero; the other fled before the Wildcats had a real chance at them.

On Henderson Field there was a brisk hustling. As fast as the mechanics, armorers and ground-service men could attend to the returning planes, and the fighter director gathered half a dozen together, to okay them for the take-off, they would set out for the enemy again. There were no longer regular squadron formations. Army, Navy and Marine fliers teamed up for the island-ship-island shuttle. Machines landed, stopped quickly, brakes hard on, turned and powered across to be reloaded. They queued up, jostled each other to get on the runway, and took off again. There weren't a large number of planes, but those in service worked fast and the Japs co-operated to the last degree by proceeding full steam toward Guadalcanal, thus shortening the flight distance with every minute.

Hoot Gibson and his buddy, Robinson, were outward bound again with one of the last formations. Since it was now only a fifty-mile hop, there was scarcely time for the bombers to gain sufficient altitude for their dives. The planes had reached only about 9000 feet when they saw the last light of the setting sun give a final burnish to the sinking enemy vessels strung out astern of the surviving ships, which continued doggedly onward.

Looking out on peaceful Michigan Avenue, in Chicago many months later, Hoot related: "Just before we got to the transports we were attacked by Zeros. Again Schimdele shot down one and smoked a second. I prepared to attack. Everything seemed normal. Then, just before I turned over, we were jumped by more Zeros. They made six or seven attack runs in rapid succession. One plastered my controls and forced me out of formation. I was in a bad spot. It's almost impossible to defend against a number of Jap fighters alone, so I immediately nosed down, hung onto my bomb to help speed my dive, and kept going until almost at sea level. I hadn't heard the rear gun shooting, so I figured the Zeros must have been shaken off. But as I flattened out and let the bomb go I was startled to see a stream of tracers flash past the wing.

"Diving down into the denser air, I had forgotten to come back from high to low blower (supercharger setting). My pressure gauge showed what I read to be insufficient pressure and I thought my engine had cut out. A couple of seconds elapsed before I realized that there was so much pressure that the needle had gone right around the dial and was climbing up the other side. I kicked the blower back into low and reduced the throttle setting. This brought the engine back to normal.

"At just about the same time I discovered why Schimdele was not shooting. His guns had jammed. With jammed rear guns, only partial control owing to the damage to the lines, and with a Jap sitting right astern, our position was nothing to be envied. The Jap stayed on my tail with engine throttled back, firing short bursts. I swung the plane violently from side to side and occasionally Schimdele would get the guns free for a couple of bursts before they'd jam again. There was no chance to turn around for a shot with the fixed bow guns either. That would only give the Zero a chance to come inside of me and get a sitter. Nothing would get me out of this fix, I figured, except to go on with the seesaw game, and hope.

"The Zero hung on, never more than a hundred and fifty yards astern, often closer. We chased across the Russel Islands, skidding and sideslipping. At last he evidently ran out of ammunition. He pulled up alongside, flew wing tip to wing tip for a few seconds, then turned outward and away. We got back to Henderson Field with all four gas tanks punctured, and the plane, especially the port side, heavily riddled with bullets."

Len Robinson had a similar experience and had to use every trick he knew to extricate himself from a persevering Zero. Len leveled out after laying his bomb on a transport and began his trip home when he was attacked fiercely by a Zero. This fast, maneuverable fighter flew rings around Len's ambling bomber and took up position above him for a series of shallow, stabbing, dive-shooting runs. To prevent the Jap from succeeding in an underside attack, Robinson hugged the surface of the sea, forcing the Zero to pull out of each overhead dive while he was still above if he wanted to avoid crashing into the sea. Len's rear gunner coolly fired just enough bullets to drive the Jap back out of range every time he attempted to close in astern. The pursuit went on until the Russels loomed up ahead. Len headed for land and then hedgehopped. He skimmed trees, went almost into the grass across clearings, zoomed over ridges and ducked into rocky gullies, trusting to brush off the Zero. Eventually the Jap ascended. It was plain he had had enough. Robinson swung his plane around, and at 5 P.M. rejoined the rest of the boys on Henderson Field.

Three other members of the same outfit were not so fortunate. They never came back.

When the last tired American flier turned his back on the Japs, the flame-gutted hulls of the enemy derelicts glowed like beacons in the deepening night and only four limping transports and three destroyers still struggled toward the Jap positions on Guadalcanal.

Bucky Lee's SBD-10 had made its final attack at dusk, and six Dauntless machines, led by Lieutenant Commander Noel Thomas, the squadron's executive officer, had been attacking the transports when Lieutenant Warren Walsh was forced down into the sea by angry flak.

Lieutenant Haney J. ("Tiny") Carroun, of Smackover, Arkansas, also suffered plane damages, but managed to get his machine some distance away before his engine packed up. He was able to make a good water landing. The plane sank, however, before he could free the raft. That left him and his gunner, Aviation Radioman Robert Hyson, floating in their Mae Wests, about thirty-five miles from the Russel group. They started to swim toward the islands but became separated during the night. Hyson has been reported missing ever since.

Carroun alternately swam and floated to husband his strength, then dozed, swam and floated some more. He was buffeted about by bumper waves, but his Mae West kept his head above water. About forty-eight hours later he had partly worked his way and been partly carried by ocean currents to a fine beach. Nearing the shore, he saw a coconut drifting past. He collected it and pushed it in front of him, much as a water polo player dribbles the ball. A second coconut caught his eye as he struggled for the shore. Gnawing hunger and thirst made him go after this one, too. Already he envisioned the cooling milk trickling down his parched throat, slaking his thirst. At last his feet touched bottom. He gather up two more coconuts floating past, and found still another. Now he was in only two feet of water. There was some surf and the undertow was dragging out to sea. He would stand up and wade in.

He strove to get to his feet, but his tired legs refused to give him support, weighed down as he was in heavy flying gear, sodden and wet. As he struggled a boiling wave seized and swept him and the coconuts off the beach, out to sea again. His food was lost, irretrievably.

Carroun drifted and dozed all through his third night at sea, but he held on to life tenaciously. His eyes were clamped shut tightly. His face, lashed by salt brine and burned by a scorching sun, was swelling beyond belief. He had lost full consciousness.

Late in the afternoon another wave gripped him, lifted him and tossed him a long distance forward. When it released him he felt himself lying in a scarce few inches of water. He strained to roll up into the dry sand. Exhaustion overcame him and he sank into a deep sleep.

Friendly natives discovered him on the sand not long after, just above tide level. They carried him to their village, fed and nursed him, and eased the swelling so that he could see again.

In a neighboring village there was a Marine aviator whom the sea had also given up, and who had also been restored to health by friendly tribesmen. The islanders brought the Marine to meet Tiny, and preparations were made to return to Guadalcanal. The tribesmen provisioned a canoe and, with the two white men, began the long paddle to Tulagi. Eventually the canoe reached Tulagi and safety.

When Commander Flatley's air group landed on Guadalcanal late in the afternoon of November 14, one of Jim's first inquiries was for Lieutenant Colonel Joe Bauer, USMC, one of Jim's old acquaintances.

Bauer was about to take off in a Wildcat to inspect the remnants of what had been the Jap transports. Already in his plane, he cut his engine when Jim ran across the field and climbed on the wing. Their greeting was warm and friendly. "Where you going, Joe?" Jim finally asked, and added with a grin, "I thought they'd make you a ground officer around here."

"That's the trouble," Bauer told him. "I'm tired of seeing the boys off all day while I stay behind. I'm going to see for myself what the convoy looks like." With a "See you when I get back," he took off. It was then about 5:15 P.M.

Colonel Bauer had satisfied himself as to the damage inflicted on the enemy and was ready to return to base when two Zeros swooped on his tail. He was able to knock off one. The second damaged his controls and forced him into the sea. Captain Joe Foss had accompanied Bauer on this mission and saw the machine settle down a few miles from the convoy. Foss flew over low to see if Bauer was all right. He wasn't. His rubber dinghy had not freed itself before the Wildcat sank. Foss dropped lower and tried to release his own boat. (Operating a lever which opens the flap of the boat pocket frees a rubberized fabric roll, which inflates automatically.) It, too, stuck tight. Wagging his wings at Bauer, who was swimming strongly by this time, Foss signaled that he was going for help. Bauer waved back, indicating he understood.

Foss hightailed it for Guadalcanal. He came straight in across the end of the strip, stormed up the runway and taxied hurriedly to the operations tent.

"Those Jap —— got Joe," he yelled. Over the telephone he reported to General Wood that Bauer was down without a boat and requested a "duck" (seaplane) to go out after him.

A minute or two later a jeep brought Major Joe Renner, USMC, operations officer under General Wood and a close friend of Joe Bauer. He called to Foss on the run: "Come on, Joe. We'll see if we can pick him up before it's too dark." To a small group gathered around Foss, he said, "I'd like four fighter pilots to volunteer as escort." Every pilot present wanted to go. Renner selected the nearest four.

The Wildcats went off into the dusk, picked up the "duck" and headed for the area where Foss had last seen Bauer. Darkness was closing down fast. They circled over the position until black night blanketed the sea.

Across the "round table" that night, Joe Bauer was uppermost in everyone's mind. Was he still swimming? . . . Headed for one of the islands? . . . Picked up by the Japanese? He had been about fifteen miles off the Russels when his plane went down and the sea around him had been littered with rafts and wreckage and Japs. Infantry, mechanics, armorers —every outfit on the island soon knew about Joe Bauer's loss, and came to see if the rumor were true. But somehow confirmation of it was not too disheartening. They knew Joe would turn up again. Tomorrow, perhaps. Didn't he always come out all right?

Talked veered to the early, bad days on Guadalcanal, when Bauer had first arrived, accompanied by only nine Wildcats. In those days the Japs still ruled the sky and sea. Bauer had set his plane down, looked over the situation, and then called his fliers together for a pep talk.

"Beginning tomorrow," he told them, "things are going to be different. We have good planes and we can fly and shoot. When the Japs come over, we'll be up there waiting for them. We'll blast them out of the sky."

The Japs came, as usual, and upstairs at 15,000 feet sat Joe Bauer and fifteen Marine fighter pilots. Lieutenant Robert Stout, flying at the rear of the formation, reported: "Zeros in force above and astern." There were twenty-one. Bauer's voice came over the intercom: "Swing around and go for them. Follow me." The Wildcats went in to meet the Nips head on. This was a new one for the Japs.

A spectacular melee developed, planes milling and maneuvering for position, twisting, turning, diving and zooming Zeros and Grummans. Planes aflame and out of control were spinning around dizzily. It was all over in a few minutes. Bauer accounted for four Zeros outright and rode the fifth into the ground. His boys destroyed the other sixteen. All of the colonel's planes returned.

Lying back in their foxholes, the ground troops had watched this magnificent performance with profound admiration. Staring up at the turmoil in the sky, they couldn't believe what they were seeing. They followed the bout blow by blow, and as the fight progressed, with Japs crumbling left and right, the men's emotions burst out in cheers and whistles, stamping and shouts. When the airmen landed, they were rushed and mobbed, and led in victorious parade to their quarters. This had been the first truly hopeful demonstration the men had seen since setting foot on the island and it instilled in them new faith. As a token of their joy and gratitude they had presented Bauer with a huge Jap flag, one of the trophies for which they had fought so hard.

On the following day, to prove that the feat could be repeated, Bauer sent four dive bombers to Japanese heaven.

So into the night one tale followed another. The story of Joe Bauer was inexhaustible.

The arrival of the *Enterprise* air group had taxed the base's scant accommodations to the limit, but as usual the Marines rose to the occasion. Not only did they share food and beer, they conjured up bunks for those of their guests who wanted them. After "Maytag Charlie" paid his usual nocturnal visit and dropped his stick of bombs, to provide the Navy fliers with the right Guadalcanal atmosphere, everyone was ready to go to sleep.

Flatley was saying good night to the Reapers when a late transport plane came in. From it emerged a limping figure whom Jim recognized at once as Bobby Edwards. Naturally, everyone was glad to see him, although they were surprised that he should be released from base hospital so soon. They had left there only four days ago. It developed that he wasn't exactly released. When one of the boys asked: "How did you get here, Bob?" Edwards drawled casually, "Oh, I heard from one of the air transport pilots that you were here, so I thumbed a ride and arrived by the plane that just came in." If unused Wildcats hadn't been so scarce, Edwards would have taken one aloft then and there to make up for the day's fighting he had lost.

Eventually everyone got to bed, most of them in foxholes, because they had not yet forgotten the previous night's shelling. Their exhausted bodies stretched out and sleep came at once. While they slept, a big naval battle was shaping up. At sunset the day before, another powerful enemy fleet of two battleships, eight or ten cruisers and many destroyers had been reported a few hours' steam off Savo Sound. Unknown to the enemy, an American naval force—including two of our newest and best battleships, 35,000-tonners, one of which was Admiral Willis A. Lee's flagship—was about eighty miles south and within easy steam of Guadalcanal. The force was waiting for darkness before approaching, so that it would not be observed by Jap watchers from their lookout posts on Guadalcanal.

Toward midnight the Japanese warships neared Savo Island. They were headed for Cape Esperance, from where they planned to send cruisers and destroyers through the north channel to shell the American shore positions. Meanwhile, the four surviving transports were to rush into Tassafaronga and unload their soldiers and supplies before dawn, because daybreak would subject them to renewed American bomber and torpedo attacks.

Three young Naval lieutenants in command of a trio of PT boats off Guadalcanal were awaiting the arrival of Admiral Lee's force. In co-operation with it, they were to participate in the expected night engagement. The hours ticked off. Ten P.M. passed and there was no sign of the American force. It began to look as though their tiny ships would be forced to take on the enemy alone.

Swift PT boats had been serving in the waters of Guadalcanal for several weeks. Their main purpose had been to harass night marauders and already their torpedoes had sunk one cruiser, six destroyers and a patrol vessel.

Waiting no longer, the three PTs went chugging out the northern channel to meet whatever was there. Each had plenty of torpedoes and was intent on spending them on the Japs, with or without support.

They were cruising northwest of Savo when the great shapes of two battleships loomed out of the darkness. They had scarcely made out the towering superstructures when cruisers and destroyers came into view, still fanned out but closing into single column to enter the channel.

The PTs deployed and prepared to attack when their radios crackled: "This is Ching Chong China Lee," and asked them if they knew who was speaking. The small boats had been seen in the dark and this was the admiral's way of identifying his force. All three PT skippers knew that Admiral Lee had spent several years on China stations. They returned his signal with, "Yes, *sir*, we sure do!" Back came the voice: "Then get out of the way. I'm coming through."

The fleet entered Savo Sound silently and turned to steam slowly westward, on a course parallel to the north shore of Guadalcanal. There the ships merged with the blackness of the shore and were hidden completely against the backdrop of Guadalcanal's mountains. A screen of sniffing destroyers nosed back and forth for possible enemy submarines.

Meanwhile, the overconfident Jap fleet had carelessly split into two groups. Two cruisers and a third ship, reported as either a battleship or heavy cruiser, passed through the northern entrance into the sound while the main force, consisting of at least one battleship, five or six cruisers and their accompanying destroyers, were some distance astern, and obviously intended to pass west of Savo. A ninety-degree left turn would bring them through the southern entrance to rejoin the first force in the sound. Some of the destroyers and a light cruiser stayed close inshore upon entering the waterway. Apparently the Japs hoped that American warships which might be present would be driven out through the southern channel by the Jap force sent in from the northern end—straight into the guns of the stronger Jap force cruising outside in readiness. But it didn't happen that way.

Navy signalmen, accompanied by Marines off duty from the Tulagi garrison, watched the drama unfold from the island's highest point. They had watched the three PT boats chug seaward, then come back again and keep going far up the channel. Next, through night glasses, they had spied Lee's ships: first the screening destroyers, the flagship, closely followed by the second battleship, some cruisers and the rear brought up by the remainder of the destroyers. The spirits of the watchers rose.

The American warships had scarcely exchanged the patches of moonlight which shone through cloud drifts for the shadows of Guadalcanal when three small vessels slunk around Savo, passing that island to the north. A watching signalman whistled through his teeth: "Boy, oh, boy! Japs! Look at that low silhouette. They're cans [destroyers]." They moved toward Guadalcanal in the moonlight. Then, abruptly, they turned and began to speed back.

"The yellow monkeys must have seen something. They're running fast," the signalman muttered.

Then three bigger ships hove into view. They had come from between Savo and Tulagi and were now well inside the sound, about halfway between Tulagi and Guadalcanal. The three Japs were about seven miles distant and on the starboard beam of our ships, which were standing out to sea, headed roughly northwest by west, a course which would take them to the open sea through the south channel between Cape Esperance and Savo Island.

The American crews had long been at battle stations. Dim battle lanterns furnished light inside the ships for the ammunition handlers, gun loaders, gun pointers, talkers and range finders. The men listened tensely to the range and

Vice Admiral William F. Halsey pins the Navy Cross on Lieutenant
Commander James H. Flatley, of Green Bay, Wisconsin, Reaper leader.
The ceremony took place at Pearl Harbor on September 30, 1942.
(*Official U. S. Navy Photo, via Press Association*)

The carrier *Enterprise* during a Japanese dive bomber attack, with Battleship "x", (So. Dakota) right beside her, throwing up an anti-aircraft barrage. (*Official U. S. Navy Photo*)

Action in the Battle of Santa Cruz, October 26. A U. S. carrier, battleship and destroyer fill the sky with anti-aircraft fire.

direction of the target, as the figures were called out over the communication system. They had already rammed the 2200-pound projectiles of the main batteries tightly into place with great drums of powder. These would be ignited and their gas would force the shells out as soon as the firing trigger clamped down. Equipped with split-second delayed contact fuses, to give the missiles time to pierce the armor plate before exploding their several hundred pounds of bursting charge, these hard, steel-encased projectiles, with their soft iron noses, would "stick" to the armor for better penetration and drill 16-inch holes. Accompanied by terrific blasts, they would detonate, cleaving steel plates, tearing down bulkheads and causing general destruction. All the gun crews required now was the range for setting the elevation of their piece and direction to point the big rifles at their target.

The range decreased rapidly as powerful engines drove the American warships along the quiet waters of the sound. Then came Admiral Lee's order to all ships: "Fire when ready," and instantly giant tongues of flames arched through the darkness. The flagship's number one turret had fired her first salvo. A star shell flashed over an enemy warship as the projectiles struck. Explosions spread huge yellow-red flares over the stricken vessel, then a brilliant mass of fire shot into the air. The flagship's number two turret stretched out for the target. Thin red tracers marked the shells' flight for the fire directing officer, high up in the fighting top. The 35,000 tons of steel fairly leaped with the recoil of each discharge, jolting the crew sharply with every new salvo. American battleships had not thus engaged the enemy since the Spanish American War, forty-four years ago.

At the time the American fleet opened fire, the enemy ships were executing a turn and were not in good fighting formation. Two vessels, passing each other, actually presented an overlapping target. American projectiles, large and small, ripped into them. One of the ships disintegrated and disappeared and two others were set ablaze within seven minutes. One sank almost at once, and the other a half hour later.

The American force was unscarred except for a single heavy shell that struck the face plate of the second battleship's after turret at the lower edge, a few inches off deck. Although the tough armor of the turret face had withstood the impact, there was some consternation. The enemy shell had been fired at such close range that its consequent almost flat trajectory had carried it low across the broad deck, clipping a hatch cover, where it exploded. The flame had carried to the battleship's seaplanes and lighted up the vessel for all to see until the fire detail could ditch the planes overboard, a dangerous task because of the exploding gasoline tanks and the fired gasoline which ran down onto the decks.

The American line had cut a great curving S course to come to the aid of a group of destroyers, and in so doing noticed a heavy cruiser close to shore and about three and a half miles astern. The vessel was making for the open sea via the southern channel.

The task of stopping this ship fell to the second battleship. Her number three gun crew, who had feared the shell hit might have harmed the massive turret's mechanism, was relieved to see it swing easily. The fire-fighting party was ordered off the after deck to escape the muzzle blasts of the big rifles and the enemy was lined up. The turret stopped turning and the three guns depressed their muzzles. There was a moment's stillness while the gun pointer aimed for the zigzagging vessel. Then the after turret let go. The blast of her powerful driving charges blew her own burning aircraft overside and extinguished the flames. The guns' second discharge stopped the Jap. He was now a sitter. Quickly reloaded, the turret moved a little more to the right. This time all three missiles struck squarely home. There was a gigantic explosion, and when the smoke cleared the cruiser was seen sinking, stern first, and Iron Bottom Bay, as Savo Sound was nicknamed, had added another hulk to its scrap pile.

Closer to Savo, our destroyers were being contained by a flotilla of enemy destroyers and a cruiser. It was a toe-to-toe struggle, with our small ships at a disadvantage because of the presence of the Jap cruiser, which heavily outgunned them. Still, they set one enemy ship aflame. One of our destroyers, too, was burning, but the rest of the vessels pressed the enemy hotly and forced the Jap into a great blunder, the discharge of his torpedoes. The enemy line wheeled and closed in to deliver the attack. Together, the ships aimed and loosed their twin, triplet and quadruplet banks of torpedo tubes mounted on the open decks. The American destroyers ordered their helms put hard over and turned their knife-sharp bows, presenting their small, 35-foot beams rather than their 335-foot hulls. Not a single hit was scored. One torpedo was seen running close to the second battleship, but a slight course alteration passed it safely astern. The enemy had wasted its destroyers' most dangerous weapon.

Admiral Lee now closed in and soon was near enough to distinguish friend from foe. He fired the guns of the flagship over his destroyers and at the enemy. As yet, the second battleship, following astern, held her fire. About this time the second of the doughty American destroyers was mortally hit.

The American battleships had scarcely entered this fight when three enemy warships, a battleship and two big cruisers, standing to the south and due west of Savo, sighted our force. One of the cruisers opened the shutters of her four searchlights, two on each mast, and played them on the *South Dakota*. To the watchers on Tulagi, it must have looked much like an open-air battle film, with the projected battleship taking the center of the stage.

The scene changed quickly. The battleship's 5- and 16-

inchers, aimed well between and below the searchlights, spoke their piece. There was instant darkness when they struck at the cruiser's midriff. Split into two sections, the cruiser sank even before our ships' secondary guns had stopped shooting.

The enemy's battleship and second cruiser remained. Admiral Lee's flagship, which had commenced firing at the dreadnaught, was unsuccessful in drawing the enemy's attention off the *Dakota*, which seemed to have been marked by the Japs as the primary target. Both battleship and cruiser kept pounding at her with their 8-inch, 6-inch and 5.5-inch guns, aiming to destroy her range-finding, battery-control equipment and secondary armament. Their 14-inch batteries were directed at her hull, and three or four other Jap cruisers, which had stood far off, unnoticed, beyond the first two warships, added their fire. Shells were falling into the sea all around, but it was the close-range shooting of the first battleship and cruiser which was hitting home, killing and wounding some of her personnel, starting small fires and wrecking or damaging parts of the secondary controls.

Slowly drifting star shells were lighting up the Jap battleship for our gunners when a second enemy cruiser sacrificed herself by turning on her four searchlights, one above the other, on each mast. There was silence aboard the battleship for a moment while her gunners made the necessary slight aiming adjustments. Then the newly aligned main batteries fired with a crashing bellow, and a few seconds later the missiles burst inside the Nip's hull. The cruiser began to burn and her flames drew fire from other American ships. Added to the devastating blows delivered by the battleship's main armament, the concentrated fire was too great for any ship to withstand. Like her sister cruiser, this one, too, was blasted in two, each battered half going down separately.

The *Dakota* was still the main target. One 1460-pound projectile struck at her armored side above the water line and another exploded with a deafening roar and a great sheet of flame against the armor aft. But as heavily as the battleship was being hit, the enemy was getting it even worse. The flagship's shells were now tearing into the Jap heavyweight and fires could be seen burning inside through gaping holes torn into her hard skin. Other fires started on her decks and in the fighting tops of her superstructure, spreading throughout the full length of her big hull. The flames soon became too fierce for her crew, and one after another, her guns stopped firing. The American vessels, seeing she was doomed, stopped shooting into the blazing mass. She burned until she, too, slid to the bottom. The surviving enemy warships and destroyers disappeared into the night, headed north.

This part of the action had lasted about twenty minutes. Admiral Lee's flagship had suffered only minor damage. The battleship's superstructure, however, had been sieved by more than thirty projectiles and our cruisers had been hit badly.

The astonishing thing about this action was that the Jap scored only two hits with his 14-inch rifles, even though the engagement lasted twenty minutes and the enemy battleship, aided by searchlights, had fired almost continuously at our battleship, whose own fires alone should have made her a good target. To hit only twice, at such close range, in that length of time, was an extremely poor display of gunnery.

The *South Dakota* crew had withstood a terrible ordeal during those twenty minutes. Between their allotted tasks of handling communications, navigation, signals and other assignments, they had fought fires, repaired broken pipes and electric wiring to maintain the ship in fighting trim, and attended to the wounded besides.

Perhaps the best picture of the battle comes from the men

themselves. Yeoman First Class Hoden Othello Patrick, a "talker" in the battleship's sky forward station, was stationed in the small topmost flat of the fighting top. With him were two officers and eleven enlisted men. Patrick had watched the flagship open fire; a split second later an enemy shell had exploded in the superstructure directly beneath his deck. The concussion threw Patrick flat and he must have lost consciousness for a few minutes.

When he revived, he was lying on his back. An arm without a body was across his face. "I thought, 'I'm dead. This is what it's like to be dead,'" he recalled later. But a sharp pain in his knee made him realize that he was much alive. Although his kneecap had been blow off, he struggled to his feet and saw that both officers were dead. Seven of the enlisted men were stretched out prone, still, and he surmised that they were dead. The other four were wounded and gazed at him in mute appeal.

Ignoring his own hurt, Patrick examined the wounded and urged the two least injured to get medical treatment below decks. The other two bled profusely and were too badly hurt to be moved. Patrick applied their belts as tourniquets and staunched the flow of blood. He used his own belt to stop the heavy bleeding from his knee wound. Next he searched for the morphine supply, which he divided carefully to give each of the two men an injection, saving some for himself.

As he finished treating his two buddies, some of the seven he had though dead moved. Selflessly, he split up his share of morphine and gave it to them. Occasionally he loosed their tourniquets and made them generally comfortable. Meanwhile, the battle went on and shells ripped into the ship. In recognition of this unselfish service, Patrick has the distinction of being the only enlisted man to be recommended for the Navy Cross. (The Navy's practice of instructing numbers of crewmen in first aid pays off extremely well.

Small metal boxes, welded to the armor at scores of stations throughout every warship assure handy supplies of morphine, tannic acid jelly for burns, and bandages.)

In the conning tower of the battleship, Rufus Mathewson, a yeoman second class and also a "talker," had been listening to the droning voice of the range finder: ". . . target 20,000 yards, bearing 240 degrees. . . . Target 19,800 yards, bearing 241 degrees . . ." and so on, as the two forces closed. Then the quiet voice of the admiral had come through: "Fire when ready." Mathewson heard a terrific concussion and, peering through a narrow slit in the conning tower's thick armor, he caught a glimpse of the flagship ahead. She had just fired and was illuminated brightly by her own muzzle flares.

His own ship jarred. Her heavies, too, had fired and the shock of their discharge jerked the men from their 'scopes. Through the phones a voice exclaimed: "Right on," meaning that the target had been hit with the first salvo. Then another voice: "The damn thing has dissolved . . . it looked like a cruiser," and a third voice interrupting: "That was a battleship."

Then another jar, followed by more severe ones. Enemy shells were exploding aboard. As each one tore into the upper works, the blasts ripped decks, tore down light steel walls and splinter curtains, and bounded back off gun housings. There was a constant jangle of steel fragments ricocheting off steel bulkheads. The tremendous friction engendered by the impact of shells on hard armor generated enough heat literally to melt steel, and molten metal could be seen running down the armor plate, fusing and solidifying in weird patterns.

In the number two control station, a duplicate of the main bridge from which the ship is steered, the executive officer, Commander Archibald E. Uehlinger, was in readiness before the first shot was fired to take over should captain and bridge be destroyed. In this station, the exec and staff can listen in over a loudspeaker to every order going to and coming from the captain. They follow every move closely so that if they have to take command in an emergency they will know exactly from what point to continue.

Commander Uehlinger and his staff were crowded into their small emergency station when a shell penetrated the adjoining steel bulkhead and cut the steam pipe leading to the ship's siren. This freed great clouds of steam which rushed into the compartment at high pressure, raising the temperature in the station to an almost unbearable point. To add to the officers' discomfort, fire had broken out in the compartment below their deck and the flames heated the steel flooring while they licked the underside. It was far from a pleasant battle station.

Bernard Wenke, on duty as emergency helmsman, had been thrown to the deck by one of the close explosions. He remembers that he retained his grip on the wheel with one hand, but as he lay there a moment, the nearly red-hot deck set fire to his pants. He suffered no more serious injuries.

The men below deck deserve the greatest admiration. In battle, they follow their tasks methodically and calmly as though nothing untoward were happening. They feel the jars of guns fired and of bursting shells, but they are so far removed that they cannot tell one from the other. They tend their boilers and engines, answer the directions of the numerous dials and the orders which come through the communicators, and occasionally hear parts of a running description of the battle by an officer observing above.

Those manning the fire and engine rooms have to be fatalists. They are surrounded by pipes carrying live steam at pressures above 600 pounds per square inch, so hot that its very nature is changed from steam to gas. In this form it becomes invisible. Leaks can only be discovered by searching with a rag attached to a long stick which bursts into flames if it is held near a leak. When this gaseous matter is brought in contact with human skin, it doesn't scald, as does ordinary steam, but rather strips flesh from bone.

Chief Yeoman Cheek had been on duty in the engine room during the action and his regular inspection showed everything functioning perfectly. His dials registered as they should and his ventilating fans circulated fresh, cool air to keep the temperature comfortable. He could hear faintly the dull vibrations of the battle raging above and outside, and could feel the ship jump when the big ones fired. Between answering requests and carrying out orders, he sat and read an old copy of *Reader's Digest*.

He was well aware of the considerable fight going on topside and was well aware of what the score would be if damage should reach below. He went on reading.

Next morning he went on deck to survey the damage and claims he was so shocked "that I didn't sleep for three nights afterward."

When the battle smoke cleared away at last, the score stood: Jap ships—two battleships, eight cruisers, six destroyers, eight transports and four cargo vessels sunk; two battleships, one cruiser and seven destroyers damaged; American ships—two cruisers and seven destroyers sunk.

The destroyer *Buchanan* had been hit by a shell from an enemy shore battery while Admiral Callaghan's cruiser force was bombarding enemy lines, supply dumps and rear positions on November 12, and failed to report after setting out for an advanced island base for repairs.

Tabulation showed further that Admiral Callaghan's cruiser force had knocked out a large proportion of the Japs, a share almost equaling the toll exacted by Admiral Lee's battleship force. The dashing attack of Callaghan's cruisers and their audacity in action will long be recounted among Navy men.

On Henderson Field, most of the Reapers had slept through the cannonade, and the great drumfire of guns and bursting shells had rolled over the sea without disturbing their slumbers. They learned of the battle and its outcome next morning, when they met other men whose duties had kept them up through the night.

Lightheartedly, they snatched a quick breakfast and started on their morning flights.

A "duck" was dispatched, escorted by some Wildcats, to search again for Colonel Bauer, and although they combed the sea for him carefully, he had vanished. Days passed, and weeks, and no word from Bauer ever came. Hope for him waned except on the part of his men, who held the belief for long after that somewhere, free or captured, he was safe and would return. From time to time one of the boys would be heard to announce that he had a new hunch, that he had just discovered another spot where "Indian Joe" might be found. Usually he would be granted permission to take his plane on another fruitless hunt. "Indian Joe" Bauer is today one of Guadalcanal's legendary heroes.

Other fighters, on the morning after the battle, flew cover for destroyers which were looking for survivors. Dive bombers, accompanied by still other fighters, went in search of damaged Japanese vessels. On the beach at Tassafaronga four transports had been run aground deliberately by their captains in a desperate effort to salvage some supplies. Decks and beach swarmed with Japs, trying frantically to get as much of the ships' cargoes ashore as possible. The bombers laid their eggs on these targets and the crash of the explosions re-echoed from the hills. Bombs and incendiary bullets set ships and dumps ablaze, while the fighters made good use of their machine guns. Bombing and Scouting 10 added their weight to the assault. During the morning one of the transports contrived to extinguish its fire and little Japs were crowding around the beached vessel like ants around a bone, hurrying the precious cargo ashore.

Hoot Gibson and Lieutenants E. J. Stevens and Ralph Goddard of Bombing 10 took on a bomb each to stop them. They had been ordered to aim for the forward end of the transport and rekindle the fire. Hoot attacked first. He laid his projectile right into the hull, just forward of the bridge. It exploded deep inside and apparently hit a store of ammunition. Explosions followed one another in rapid succession and fires quickly enveloped the entire ship. That took care of the vessel. Goddard selected the next best target, a large mass of supplies stacked on the beach, in the center of which he saw an interesting ridge. He dived and his bomb landed flush center. It started the biggest fire ever seen on Guadalcanal, and by the time Goddard returned to the flying field the Army lookout had reported a conflagration which spread to an area half a mile long and several hundred yards wide. It must have been one of the main gasoline and ammunition dumps the Japs had cached on the island.

Then came warning of the approach of hostile planes. Stan Ruehlow, Bobby Edwards (in spite of his cracked knee-cap), and six other Reapers were launched from Henderson Field. They climbed rapidly to intercept. Commander Flatley and his section, already in the air for several hours, also climbed and prepared to fight, although they conserved their gasoline carefully and intended to keep within gliding distance of Henderson Field, in case their tanks should run dry during combat.

The first sight contact with the enemy was made at 3:20 P.M. An advance guard of eleven Zeros approached at 20,000 feet. Their bombers followed far astern. Stan Ruehlow's flight, closely followed by Bobby Edwards' four, intercepted the Zeros above Savo Island. At the same time Jimmy's section closed with the enemy from another angle. The Japs had two strikes on them before the first shot was fired. They were eleven and had to face twelve Reapers. Seldom had the Reapers met the foe with anything approaching even numbers. This time they actually outnumbered the enemy.

The battle could end only one way. Six Zeros were shot down, four damaged, the eleventh fled and the Jap bombers did an about-face so that they would live to fight another day.

There were no real casualties among the Reapers, although Dave Pollock had engine trouble and made a splashy landing in the sea off Guadalcanal. He hit his forehead on the instrument panel and got a minor gash.

Bobby Edwards, injured knee and all, celebrated his return to the squadron by shooting down three Japs, and strafed Jap ships and troops later that afternoon.

The Reapers spent another night on Henderson Field— a peaceful night this time. The following morning, November 16, Edwards and Ruehlow took two sections of Reapers aloft to go back after the beached transports, supply dumps and any Japs they could find. For almost an hour they patrolled, chased the Japs off the water, across the beach, and pursued any group they could see. They did not return to the field until they had emptied their machine guns.

Reports from the long-range scouts indicated that there were no signs of Jap vessels within three hundred miles of Guadalcanal. The war in the Pacific appeared to have quieted down temporarily, and since no immediate excitement was in the offing, the Reapers were recalled to their base. Bad weather delayed their departure until the following day.

To while away the time, Major Duke Davis invited Flatley and some of the others to have a look around the American-held territory of Guadalcanal. Jeeps brought them close to the front lines, where they got out and walked. A few hours spent in wandering around the front, chatting with Army and Marine infantrymen, gunners and members of the hospital corps, gave the fliers a fairly clear picture of the dangers and difficulties ground troops face.

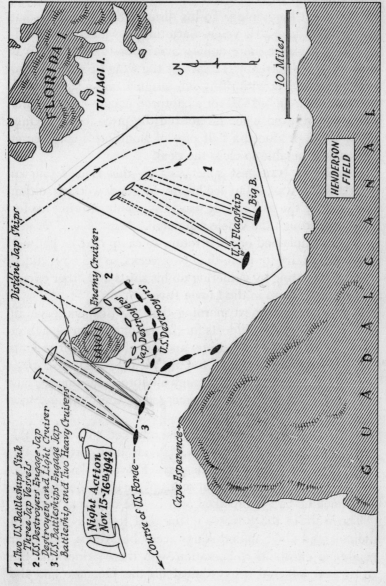

FLORIDA I.

TULAGI I.

10 Miles

HENDERSON FIELD

Distant Jap Ships

Enemy Cruiser

2

Jap Destroyers

U.S. Destroyers

SAVO I.

U.S. Flagship

Big B.

1

3

Cape Esperence

Course of U.S. Force

Night Action Nov. 15th 1942

1. Two U.S. Battleships Sink Three Jap Vessels
2. U.S. Destroyers Engage Jap Destroyers and Light Cruiser
3. U.S. Battleships Engage Jap Battleship and Two Heavy Cruisers

G U A D A L C A N A L

Night Action, November 15-16, 1942

It appeared to be a good time to collect souvenirs; Jim Flatley went bargaining. To his dismay, he discovered that money itself had little value. Bartering was much more welcome. There were more dollars than goods and no one was keen to amass currency. To saw off the wing tip of a crashed Jap plane, replete with rising sun insignia, was a simple matter, but when he bid $20 for a captured enemy flag, his offer was scorned, even when he hoisted the price to $100. Only when Duke produced a half pint of Bourbon from a secret pocket was he able to close the deal.

One of the strangest spectacles on this Cook's tour of Guadalcanal was a Jap ice plant, in good working order, captured by the Marines. It was busy manufacturing ice for the boys through the whole campaign.

Duke complained on their return to camp that he had not had any laundry for more than two weeks, so the boys ended their day's outing by gathering up his shirts and other effects and washing them in the Lunga River.

It was arranged next morning that the Reapers leave all except four of their Wildcats for the use of the Marine fighter pilots. Flatley, Whitte, Reiserer and Ruehlow took off and ran into bad weather en route, forcing them to climb to 12,000 feet. Still they had to bore through an uproarious storm. They kept going until they finally emerged in the clear and saw their goal ahead.

Bobby Edwards, who had been returned to hospital the evening before, was taken back by air transport with the remainder of the planeless Reapers. Edwards' knee was so bad that when he climbed out of his plane after the last strafing attack he had to be taken over by the doctor at once.

The work of the Reapers in the past few days had been difficult and their undertakings were hazardous, but their combined efforts in co-operation with the Marines and the Army had inflicted heavy defeat on the Japanese and the boys felt it had been well worth while. It was a relaxed and content squadron that reunited with the others ashore.

They were shooting the breeze after dinner when there came the mighty roar of a low-flying plane. It was the scout bomber which had left Guadalcanal about the same time they had, but was late in arriving. Lieutenant Doan Carmody stepped out of the craft, and from the rear seat rose Liska, who had flown with Leppla during the Coral Sea fight. He had been left without a pilot when Leppla transferred to the Reapers. Moved over to Bombing 10, he had been teamed up with Carmody. This had kept the Liska-Leppla combination together aboard the same ship until that October day, at the Battle of Santa Cruz, when Leppla was lost in combat.

Liska's deadly gunnery had since shot down two more Nips, and the flight from Guadalcanal had given him the opportunity to perform another notable feat. As his squadron passed over San Cristobal, the savage storm had separated Carmody from the others. In addition, their radio had gone out and there they were, without contact, flung about in the gale and the steadily increasing darkness. They might have been lost if it had not been for imperturbable Liska, who dismantled the radio and discovered the root of the trouble. He rebuilt the set, and conned the plane safely through to a night landing.

D. K. Liska is representative of scores of back-seat fliers in bombers and torpedo planes, who are excellent shots, first-class radiomen, and know what to do in the clinches.

Chapter 10

ONE DAY'S BATTLE

THE BATTLE of Lunga Point was the last major effort on the part of the Japs to reinforce their weakening position on Guadalcanal. American guns and aircraft had conclusively fought the enemy to a standstill. Either he would have to risk all his resources to regain the entire island, or he would have to give it up altogether. The previously arrogant Jap swallowed the bitter pill and made his decision. He chose to admit defeat and made attempts to withdraw his once numerous land army.

But here, too, American air and sea superiority in the lower Solomons forced the Japs to send in destroyers under cover of night, load their decks with troops and flee as fast as their engines could propel them before daylight came.

Our warships, steaming along Guadalcanal's shores, made the wait uncomfortable for the enemy on and near the escape beaches, and our fliers spent hours every day strafing the Japanese camps, while our ground troops successfully pushed ahead, winning new territory and encircling enemy rear-guards.

The Japs had little choice of retreat from their island position. Until their destroyers could pick them up and carry them off to bases in the northern Solomons, the best they could hope for was to find temporary safety in the rugged terrain. While there, tightly bottled up, they were forced to maintain strong air squadrons against our surface ships, to prevent them from moving in and completely cutting their sea lane. Scores of these enemy aircraft were destroyed by our fliers and ship gunners.

In January the Reapers were living in Quonset huts and tents on an island southeast of Henderson Field, where the Marines had established an advanced base. The lull of the past few weeks had enabled the air squadrons to stretch out and relax.

They were installed near a fighter strip on part of a former coconut plantation, and they had as companions members of various Marine fighter squadrons en route to and from Guadalcanal, or on their way to and from Sydney, Australia, where they were sent on leave.

Coconut plantations are natural airfields after a double row of palms is removed for the length needed and a thin layer of soil is dug up to bare the coral beneath. These coral beds are soft enough to be smoothed off with a road grader, and because they are porous, they drain off all rain as soon as it falls, making ideal landing strips. The surrounding palms furnish plenty of shade, and at the same time help to hide the planes from enemy scouts.

Plantations are treated with respect and thinned out only when and where necessary. The Allied governments, who compensate the plantation owners for use of their sites, impress upon the occupying troops that a coconut palm does not begin to bear until it is seven years old.

The French owner of the Reapers' station became particularly friendly with the boys, and although he, like all other inhabitants, had difficulty in procuring varieties of foodstuffs and delicacies, it was his delight to draw to the fullest extent upon whatever he did have stored for the airmen's pleasure. He had an excellent wine cellar, and until his stock began to give out he served wine with dinner every night. The dinners were usually lavish, eight-course affairs, made interesting by French ingenuity. Game was plentiful and the coast teemed with quantities of excellent fish. It was a Pacific Eden.

The Marines had erected a clubhouse and there were pro-
visions for open-air movies. There was also a small ice plant
and a rivet cooler served as icebox. Limes were abundant and
ice-cooled limeades were consequently available, as well as
the nutritious milk from green coconuts. "But there was
always a heavy drag on coffee," Jim Flatley says.

The camp was close to the ocean, where the Reapers swam
and fished. Behind the fighter strip there was a deep swimming hole. The water flowed from volcanic springs into a
pool a hundred and fifty feet deep; its temperature was
always about sixty degrees. It was fine, fresh water, over-
flowing into the sea. There were diving platforms, and from
overhanging branches, swinging ropes trailed to the pool.
This Elysian spot came nearest to the Reaper's dreams of a
South Sea paradise; it lacked only Dorothy Lamour to be
complete.

For exercise, the boys were in the habit of swimming about
a hundred and fifty yards up the stream to where it widened
out. There they would sport about under a small waterfall
during the hottest part of the day, when the thermometer
climbed as high as ninety-five degrees. The climate was
healthy. Flies were the only pests, but the fliers learned to
keep their mouths shut tight at the right times. There were
no malaria mosquitoes and the drinking water was excellent.
The natives were extremely friendly and did most of the
work. They were courteous and enjoyed saluting every man
who wore a uniform. Every salute had to be carefully returned, or they would feel slighted.

To do their full stint of training each day, the Reapers
arranged their schedules so they could begin flying at dawn,
stop work from about 11 A.M. to 2:30 P.M., then keep at it
again until an hour before dark.

"Living under such ideal conditions, with no greater
danger to face than coconuts dropping from fifty-foot
heights," Jim Flatley recalls, "we were shocked back into

sudden realization. We had been sitting around until midnight, sampling some Australian 'Black Death' when we heard the sound of a plane, but thought little of it because aircraft frequently came overhead at night. We were entirely removed from the main base, and took no notice until the sound of the gliding plane began to build up.

"Then we heard the unmistakable hiss of a falling bomb, followed by an explosion. The first dropped some distance away, the succeeding one came closer, and by the time the fifth had dropped, we were dashing for the slit trenches. We had learned at Guadalcanal that bombs couldn't be sneezed at, and about twenty of us jumped for a foxhole that wouldn't hold two. The result was a pile of scrambled bodies. The seventh bomb dropped very near and the eighth should have fallen on top of us because we were in direct line, but seven appeared to be all the pilot had. The Jap had come a long way and his 100-pound bombs had been a fair load to tote this far. Grinning foolishly, we unsorted ourselves and soothed our egos by ribbing each other about who had started this stampede. Next day, however, we set out with picks and spades to excavate personal shelters.

"The raid had done no actual damage. Most of the missiles had fallen about a hundred yards apart across empty country and only the final two had exploded just inside the plantation. This bombing gave us the incentive we needed. We had been doing some night flying, but for the next ten days we did all our flying at night, against the time when we might get a chance to go after these night marauders.

"Scarcely a day passed that I didn't get requests from Reapers to arrange for them to take their planes to Guadalcanal for a few days of fighting. They were spoiling for another crack at the Japs. Unfortunately, this couldn't be allowed, because we never knew when orders might come through to take off and join our carrier."

Dave Pollock had declared himself the number one fisherman and became obsessed with the idea of hooking a shark. He used dynamite caps fitted to the end of long poles for his lethal bait. Fishing at night, he lost his gear several times to big sharks and in desperation went aboard an anchored ship in the harbor and had the blacksmith fashion him the granddaddy of all hooks. This he attached to a chain leader, and in turn to a 38-cord manila rope. That afternoon he got himself a big piece of meat, laid the baited line out, and attached it to a tree. He selected a long, stout limb with plenty of spring. The result was an automatic fisherman.

Dave returned to base, excited, and invited the crowd to come down after the movie and watch him haul his shark ashore. He could scarcely sit out the picture. They restrained him till it was over and then trooped down to the ocean. The tree was still there and so was the limb. But the shark had come and gone. He had swallowed the hook, but even a heavy manila line had not been strong enough to hold him. Poor Dave's arms couldn't reach far enough to show how long the shark must have been that got away. This experience whetted his ambition and he tried again and again, but like the deer he never shot, the sharks kept one jump ahead of him.

"We were enlightened by our Marine buddies about the advantages of being a Marine," Flatley says. "Mostly because you were a Marine, it seemed, you got a trip to Sydney every so often, especially if you had flown from Guadalcanal. There was always much speculation among the Marines awaiting transport as to how much money it would be advisable to take along to finance them comfortably for a month, their period of leave. Estimates varied, but they were assured by those who had already been there that Australian hospitality would never let them down, and they would find homes and towns thrown wide open to them. Exaggerated talk had it that after two or three weeks in Sydney the boys were anxious to return to Guadalcanal so they could look forward to another stay with the Aussies."

On the subject of Joe Foss, Jim says: "It was always a big day when Joe arrived. I had known him in the early days, before he shot down twenty-six Jap planes. He was learning to fly at Pensacola at that time. I met him again in San Diego in June 1942, just after I got back from the Coral Sea. Joe was very unhappy. He had been assigned to heavy planes and was trying hard to get into fighters. He wanted to apply for admittance to the Navy fighter school at San Diego, but first he had to overcome some Marine Corps objections. Even when consent was granted, he was told that he could attend classes only on condition that they did not interfere with his routine work in big boats. When he finally got that far he discovered that classes were filled and no new students could be taken in. Laying siege to the Navy officer in command of the fighter school, he was admitted at last and passed the course without difficulty. He got his first break when the Marines gathered a fighter squadron to send to battle and Joe was among those selected.

"The Reapers, eager to get all the latest information from Guadalcanal's front lines, plagued Joe whenever he stopped over with ceaseless questions, which he answered willingly and patiently. Guadalcanal was the place from which every fighter pilot wanted to operate, and so the Marines generally were pumped dry before they were allowed to relax."

As the number of aircraft assigned to the Reapers' base grew, the boys were transferred to the bomber base, and operated from there with the other number 10 air groups. They had considerable gunnery practice.

"Our camp was commanded by my good friend Colonel Oscar Brice, USMC," Jim says. "When Oscar was ordered to Guadalcanal as operations officer before Christmas, he offered me the use of his tent, which I shared with Major William K. Pottinger, who commanded the flying strip. Pottinger, one of the outstanding Marine fighter pilots, was later relieved by Colonel Lawson H. ("Sandy") Sanderson, who moved in after having been operations officer on Guadalcanal for three months."

During these weeks Admiral Halsey had been pushing troops, supplies and equipment into the Solomons without any Jap naval interference. His masterful handling of the American forces kept the enemy well in check.

The Reapers joined a carrier occasionally and steamed out for a short cruise to cover transports going to and from Guadalcanal, but they didn't see action against the Japanese until the end of January.

On January 28 they got orders to report to a carrier. Their assignment was again routine—to cover transports—but late on January 29, their second evening at sea, a startling message came in asking for fighters to protect the cruiser *Chicago* from hostile torpedo plane attacks. They were surprised at the tenor of the request, because they understood that the *Chicago,* which had moved up with a task force to stop the Japs from evacuating Guadalcanal's beaches, had defending carrier plane protection. A second message, however, enlarged on the first report and explained that the *Chicago* and other warships had been on patrol shortly before sundown when they were subjected to the first night torpedo plane attack ever executed by the Japs. She and the other cruisers had steamed out of air range of their attending carrier, so they were without fighter plane defense at the time. The enemy had secured one torpedo hit on the *Chicago* and she was being towed by one of her destroyer escorts. They were near Rennel Island, about a hundred and twenty miles south of Guadalcanal, and would be within range of Jap twin-engined torpedo planes all through the next day.

Between dusk and dawn, our carrier was brought to within sixty miles of the *Chicago*. Detailed to provide fighter cover, a section of Reapers took off before dawn. "It was still dark," Flatley relates, "so I ordered a rendezvous above Rennel. We climbed into the first morning glow and headed for Indispensable Reefs. We located the wounded *Chicago* without difficulty. Surrounded by a destroyer screen, she was being towed by a Navy tug which had arrived during the night to relieve the destroyer. The force was proceeding slowly to the southeast. We were well inside the range of Jap bombers and expected an early morning attack. It never materialized. About noon the major portion of the force increased speed and left the *Chicago*. Some destroyers and a corvette remained behind.

"There was no sign of a Jap machine all morning. The suggestion had been that we would be joined by fighters from other carriers in the vicinity, or from Guadalcanal. When they didn't arrive, the fighters took off at time intervals to relieve the planes in the air, which then returned to the carrier and refueled, to be ready for a fast take-off if the Japs should approach."

Six Reapers—Killer Kan, Ed Coalson, Ensign M. N. ("Wick") Wickendoll, Ensign A. G. ("Cowboy") Boren, Hank Leder and Ensign Frank Donahoe—were on patrol shortly after 4 P.M. when a message from a patrol reported that twelve twin-engined Jap bombers had been sighted at high altitude in the northwestern Solomons, course 150. A quick look at the chart indicated that they were headed for the *Chicago* and would arrive about four-thirty. Six additional Reapers were launched, led by Lieutenant MacGregor Kilpatrick, to fly over the *Chicago*. Flatley, accompanied by three more Reapers, was already at 18,000 feet, covering the carrier.

At four-ten Killer's section spotted one twin-engined Mitsubishi approaching from the northwest. Wickendoll, Boren, Leder and Donahoe immediately gave chase, while Kan and Coalson stayed above the *Chicago*. As soon as the Wildcats closed in the Jap turned, opened his engines wide and tried to outdistance them. The American planes, however, enjoyed a small speed advantage of perhaps ten miles per hour, and taking long-range 800-yard shots, they were able to damage one engine, which slowed the Jap sufficiently to let the Reapers overhaul him. From then on it was a race to see which one would make the kill. Hank Leder won. He bored in to point-blank range and gave one effective burst. The Mitsu flamed and dropped into the sea. With the gas in their tanks depleted by the long chase, this section then returned to the carrier.

Kilpatrick's six-plane section arrived over the *Chicago* at about four-fifteen and relieved Kan and Coalson, who were also low on fuel. Jim Flatley, who wanted to take his section in the direction from which the twelve Japs were expected, asked for another patrol to be launched to take his place above the carrier. This was done and Flatley's section set out at about four-thirty. At that moment Kilpatrick sighted the enemy planes. They were Mitsubishis, type 1, fast (about 300 miles per hour), heavily armed and equipped with cannon in the tail, bow, waist and on top.

The Japs were down to 8000 feet when sight contact was made. They passed up the crippled *Chicago* and went for the carrier, before Kilpatrick disposed his fighters on either side of the Jap formation. Flash Gordon, Rip Slagle, Steve Kona and Whitey Feightner were placed on the outside to starboard, where they would be between the Japs and the carrier, and Bob Porter and Kilpatrick stationed themselves inside to port.

Caught in a pincer and sensing destruction, the Japs made a 150-degree turn—although their target, the carrier, was now only seventeen miles away—and headed for the *Chicago* instead, taking what they thought was the easiest way out.

Having approached in a broad V, with their about-face the Japs now formed into two six-plane Vs, one directly astern of the other. This shift caused Gordon, Slagle, Kona and

Feightner to turn around in order to overtake them.

Not absolutely certain of the Japs' intentions, Gordon didn't order the switch executed at once, but waited a few seconds to be sure they were not trying a trick in the hope of getting his section to commit itself in a dive during which the enemy torpedo planes could whip around once again and go after the carrier.

Thus, when Gordon's section finally did turn, three of the four were too far off to catch the fleeing Japs. The fourth, Feightner, had developed engine trouble and had dropped behind in the chase. He now crossed over and joined Kilpatrick. Porter and Kilpatrick attacked the enemy formation, and on the first pass, each set a Mitsu on fire. They came up and went in a second time. Again Kilpatrick fired a machine and Porter damaged another. That made three down with nine to go, and one of the nine was damaged and dropping back.

At that time Jim Flatley was twenty miles away at 18,000 feet and the first intimation he had of the fight was the sight of the bombers Kilpatrick had downed plunging, burning, through the clouds. Followed by Reiserer, Whitte and Shonk, he attained a speed well above 400 miles per hour in his gliding approach and succeeded in intercepting the leading enemy V just as it was entering the AA ring of the *Chicago* and her destroyers. The Japs had nosed down to bring their planes about two hundred feet above the water for the torpedo drop, but were still much too far out to let their missiles go. There were now seven Wildcats against nine Mitsubishis.

Feightner, who was having his first shot at the enemy this day, collected three Japs. Whitte and Flatley bagged one each and Reiserer closed in and took another, so that only five Japs remained by the time they were within torpedo range. They dropped the fish on their runs toward the ships.

After loosing the torpedoes the Japs stayed almost at water level to maintain their greatest speed and to prevent the

Wildcats from diving at them. This way the fight developed into an action where all the machines were flying horizontally, with throttles wide open. Relieved of their heavy torpedoes, the Mitsus were exceptionally fast and it required every horse in the Wildcats' engines to overtake them.

One of the Mitsus fell victim to the Reapers when he zoomed slightly to clear the fleet. Two of the remaining four were brought down within four hundred yards after they had crossed the *Chicago*. Of the remaining two, one, badly damaged, is presumed to have flopped into the sea before he got very far out. Only one can be assumed to have escaped.

Of the torpedoes dropped, one found its way to the crippled *Chicago*. She took on a heavy list and had to be abandoned. Forty-five minutes later she rolled over and sank.

When he pulled out of the chase Jim Flatley found himself bracketed by the AA fire of his own ships. The gunners' aim was perfect—except that it was directed against the wrong plane. They corrected their mistake in time and all the Reapers got back aboard safely.

The table for the day's short battle showed that the Reapers had shot down twelve planes, damaged one, and were credited with eight assists. ("Assists" are credits given to fliers for having shot at Jap planes. It is often difficult, when more than one machine attacks, to determine who actually fires the shot which downs the enemy. Sometimes, while a man silences the rear gunner in his first pass and then pulls up to make his second run, another plane darts in and pours out a burst that sends the machine down. For that reason, every man who puts a burst into an enemy plane gets an "assist," although naturally he can't be credited with having actually destroyed the enemy.)

The Reapers did not lose a single plane in bringing down the twelve enemy machines, and only one Wildcat was damaged badly enough to be turned in for repairs. It was flying again the next morning.

Chapter 11

A REAPER'S FAREWELL

In FEBRUARY the Reapers spent a short period aboard their carrier, cruising in the vicinity of Guadalcanal. There was no action and the enemy failed to offer opposition. Our land forces had broken up the last Japanese army units, and on February 11, just six months and five days after our initial landing on Guadalcanal, the Navy issued this communique: "All organized enemy resistance on Guadalcanal has ended. Operations now consist of patrols mopping up scattered enemy units." The skill, pugnacity and courage of our combined forces had pushed back the Japs at last.

The Japanese, on paper, should have won the campaign. Their carefully worked out plans fell through probably because of their inability to adjust themselves quickly to unexpected situations. Their time table, encompassing San Cristobal after their establishment of an air base on Guadalcanal, and from there reaching to the New Hebrides and further, would undoubtedly have been run off with precision had it not been for the American seizure of the airfield on Guadalcanal on August 7, 1942. Obviously, no stock answer had been worked out in advance to meet this unanticipated interference and a frantic series of abortive moves to save face took the place of a well-thought-out campaign which might have thwarted our own efforts and stopped our plans from reaching fruition.

In their overzealousness to recapture the strategic position on Guadalcanal, the Japs foolishly continued coming in to the same target month after month and thereby exposed and enabled us to nibble away at their warships, gradually denuding their fleet of essential vessels in those waters. So many enemy ships had been sunk or seriously damaged that the Japs could no longer meet us on equal terms without drawing on their last line of defense—the Jap home fleet. Japan had lost much of her amphibious mobility and was forced to anchor more closely to her island bases. Our Navy took over the initiative and held it.

With the end of the Guadalcanal campaign, Commander Flatley got new orders. They requested his return to the United States to take over command of a new carrier air group. His Reapers had been battle-tested and the air combat tactics he had developed and instilled in his fighting men had been proven in battle. The Reapers had well applied the lessons he taught them and were now able to carry on in an established pattern. Jim had forged another tough band of fighters and his job, well done, had come to an end. The Reapers had battle experience of their own to draw on now; Jim's knowledge and teachings would be of greatest value if they were transferred to less well experienced candidates. His important task now was to create more and more new squadrons of fighting men.

When Jim called his comrades together and informed them of his new assignment, the Reapers were torn between joy and pride over his promotion and sorrow for his departure. They had lived and worked as a closely knit team and everyone felt the impending separation deeply. In Jim they had not only a highly competent and respected leader, but a liked and trusted friend. When it came time for him to follow his gear over the side, he did not make a speech. Instead, he once more wrote a note, one of farewell this time, and according to his instructions, it was brought out and read after his ship had shoved off. It read:

"I can't find it in me to make a farewell speech. I'm afraid I'd get all choked up.

"I want you to know that I take my leave of you with deep regret. No squadron commander, anywhere, has ever had a gang like you serving with him. I'm so darn proud and fond of every one of you that my heart's about to bust. If I could have the pick of the Navy for my relief, it would have been the 'Killer.' (Kan had been appointed to take over Flatley's job.)

"Take care of yourselves. Stick together and don't forget to respect that airplane. Every time you see a Jap, remember Leppla, Mead, Rhodes, Caldwell, Davis, Fulton, Barnes, Miller, Edwards and Von Lehe." (These were Reapers lost or missing, most of them in combat. Miller, Edwards and Von Lehe were lost operationally. Mead and Rhodes have since been reported as prisoners of war in Japan.

"One parting word of advice. There is a definite tendency on the part of every one of you to throw caution to the winds every time you meet the enemy. We've been lucky so far. But it's dumb. We've spent hours and hours on tactics, designed not only to destroy, but also to protect ourselves. Keep that thought foremost in your minds. Rip 'em up and down, but do it smartly.

"I trust our paths will cross in the near future. Meanwhile, keep your chins up and don't forget that little guy who called himself

"REAPER LEADER"

Memorandum from Commander Flatley for The Grim
Reapers.

Subject: Your Daily Prayers.

Reference: Your Christian Background.

*(The first part of this memorandum is incorporated in the main
body of the book, on pages 121 to 123)*

        ❋   ❋   ❋   ❋

In all of us is the desire to live. It surmounts every other desire.
However, we all must die sooner or later. We are fighting now,
not so much for our own lives, but for the lives of our entire nation, for our fathers and mothers, sisters and brothers, our children, for all the millions of Americans who did not ask for this
war; who are depending on us; who are daily making sacrifices;
who are doing their part to help; who are fighting in all parts of
the world for the same thing we are fighting for. As Christians,
we should believe that a return to God, through the medium of
a few simple prayers, sincerely and humbly said, with a belief
in their efficacy, will aid us not only to attain Heaven, but will
also strengthen us to fearlessly meet and destroy our enemies.
Therefore, it is the duty of everyone of us to resort to God. If
need be, to humble ourselves by appealing to Him, who is all
kind and all just and whose one desire is that He may have us
with Him in Heaven some day.

The enclosure contains a few simple prayers common to all
Christian religions. Don't be afraid to say them. Write home and
tell our mothers we're saying them. She taught them to us when

we were knee-high. She is praying to the same God for our safety right this minute. If we don't like these prayers, say those we know and do like, but pray.

Pray for strength to do our duty as fighting men. Pray for victory. Pray for forgiveness.

The purpose of all this is not to make sissies out of us. Quite the contrary. Its purpose is to make us strong and resolute. To explain to us in some way what we are fighting for.

This is not a game. This is the most serious business of our lives. Appealing to God will strengthen and benefit us. Therefore, it is our solemn duty.

May God bless all of us and hasten our victory.

Signed.   JAMES H. FLATLEY, Lt. Comdr. U.S.N.

*   *   *   *

RECOMMENDED PRAYERS

Our Father, Who art in Heaven, Hallowed be Thy name. Thy Kingdom come, Thy will be done on earth as it is in Heaven. Give us this day our daily bread and forgive us our trespasses, as we forgive those who trespass against us, and lead us not into temptation but deliver us from all evil for Thine is the Kingdom, the Power, and Glory forever and ever.   Amen.

Dear God, give us strength to lead a good life, to face the dangers that confront me with courage and fortitude secure in the knowledge that I am fighting for the right of free men to live as Christians.

Dear God, look down with favor upon my loved ones, and give them all the blessings they need to carry on.

Oh my God, I am heartily sorry for having ever offended Thee. Forgive me and teach me to love you. I resolve never to offend Thee again, not only because sin displeases Thee, but because some day I wish to be in Heaven with Thee.

Dear God, in Your divine wisdom, aid and guide the political and military leaders of the United Nations in order that victory may be attained in the shortest possible time.

God have mercy on our fighting men wherever they may be. Strengthen them to face death unflinchingly.

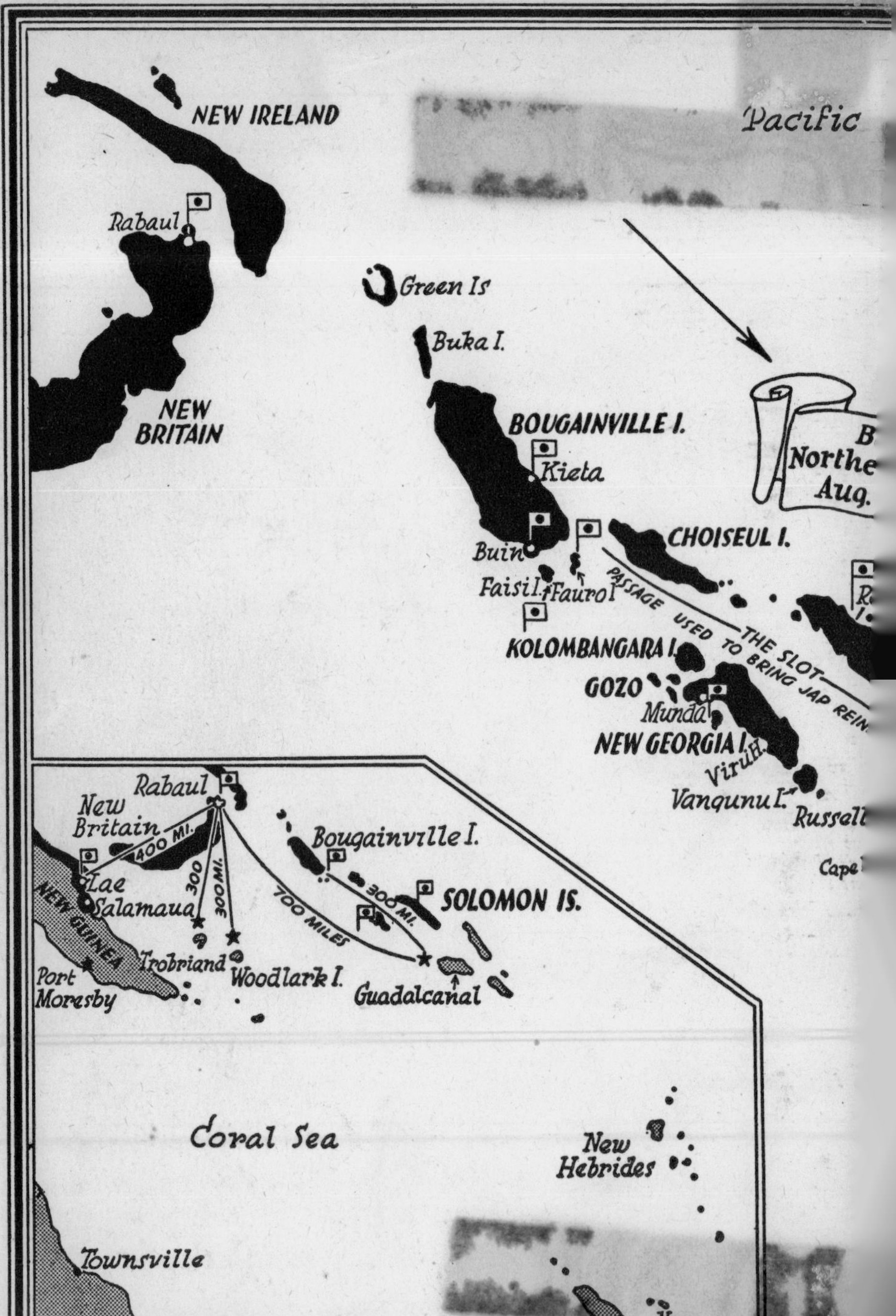
NEW IRELAND
Pacific
Rabaul
Green Is
Buka I.
NEW BRITAIN
BOUGAINVILLE I.
Kieta
Buin
CHOISEUL I.
Faisi I.
Fauro I
THE SLOT
KOLOMBANGARA I.
GOZO
Munda
NEW GEORGIA I.
Viru H.
Vangunu I.
Russell
Cape
Rabaul
New Britain
400 MI.
Lae
Salamaua
NEW GUINEA
300
300 MI.
700 MILES
Bougainville I.
300 MI.
SOLOMON IS.
Trobriand
Woodlark I.
Port Moresby
Guadalcanal
Coral Sea
New Hebrides
Townsville
AUSTRALIA
New Caledonia